HIDDEN MESSAGES
by
Maxine Taylor

First Printing 1982
Second Printing 1988
ISBN Number: 0-86690-044-06
Library of Congress Catalog Card Number: 82-072531

Published by:
American Federation of Astrologers, Inc.
P.O. Box 22040, 6535 South Rural Road
Tempe, Arizona 85282

Printed in the United States of America

This book is lovingly dedicated to

> *Joyce, my teacher, who showed me the way*
> *and*
> *Ken, my mirror, who showed me myself*

TABLE OF CONTENTS

INTRODUCTION

Women marry their fathers and men marry their mothers. We marry them, and then we try to change them. We try to make them give us the love we never got as children. Then, when they don't, we punish them, just as our parents punished each other.

We're looking for unconditional love. Most of us never got it. When we fall in love we think, ''Now, finally, here is someone who will give me the (unconditional) love I've always wanted.''

So we marry. Then it starts because we discover that no one can give us unconditional love. Why? Because we're not programmed to it. We're programmed, instead, to duplicate our parents' relationship.

How can we attract what we're not programmed to receive? If there's no tape for it? If we've never had it? We can't — until we take a conscious look at what it is we're programmed to attract. Only then can we change our lives.

This book is designed to help us to do just that.

PROGRAMMING

She was an extremely beautiful woman in her mid-thirties. She was also an extremely successful business woman — equal to or better than many men in her profession. She'd come to me for a consultation because she was considering remarrying. Although her two previous marriages had been unsuccessful, she longed for a man with whom she could be happy. She was in my office because she honestly wondered if that were possible.

In the course of the consultation, she shared that her mother had been married several times. Each time my client married, her mother encouraged her to leave her husband. Double message: **marry, but don't stay married**. As a child, my client saw her mother win every argument with each of her husbands. Message: **argue with men and win**. My client's father was strong, but distant and unaffectionate. Message: **men are distant and unaffectionate**. My client felt unloved by her husbands. Each of her stepfathers put up a good fight, but ultimately, they left. Message: **men will give up and leave**. Her mother was successful in her career. Message: **be a success in your career**.

The combination of verbal and non-verbal messages produced a woman who resented men, yet kept turning to them to make her happy. Because she was programmed for marriage to be stormy and men to leave her, she attracted just that. She married strong men and wound up emasculating them. She was looking for love, but her programming would not let her keep it.

Her fiancé played right into the program. He was stubborn and determined. He was not a success in his career, although he had potential to be. Each time he came close to success, he'd fall short. His ambitions were high, but he became a dilettante. He made a great impression, but had no money. His programming explained it all. His father had been very important in his career at one time. When the young man was just a boy, his father had been nominated for an extremely prestigious international award. Winning this award would have meant financial security for the rest of his life, as well as enormous recognition. Unfortunately, another nominee won the award. From that point on, the son was programmed to **come close, but fall short**, and that's exactly what he did in every area of life.

His parents had not gotten along. His proud, stoic father had given him the message that **the woman should put the man first**. He also felt that **men were more intelligent than women**.

These two were made for each other. Here was a chauvinist up against an aggressive woman; a loser up against a winner. When faced with a situation like this, the first reaction might be to discourage a marriage, since it seems doomed to failure before it begins. Yet, these two people were attracted to each other precisely because they could give each other what each was programmed to receive.

This scene is replayed daily all over the world. Like hamsters on a treadmill, we plug in our tapes without being aware of what they are saying. The messages run so deep and are so much a part of our subconscious habit patterns that we play right into them without realizing it.

For example, if you are programmed so that you cannot be happy while a family member is unhappy, you will find that you are never happy, because there is always someone who needs your help. Even if you are miles away, just knowing that a parent might be unhappy about some little thing can upset you. A major problem can ruin your day. After awhile, no one in the family needs to be unhappy. The mere suggestion of happiness in your life will make you unhappy. You feel guilty for enjoying yourself knowing that someone in your family might need your help. You are programmed. The minute you start to feel good you have to feel bad.

Another example: if you have been told, by word or deed, that you will never be as good as your father, then you will never be as good as your father. You will see to it that you fall short so as not to surpass him. If he has not been much of a success in his life, where does that leave you?

Sometimes we see through these messages and make a conscious decision **not** to act like our parents, **not** to buy the program. While we are still responding to the program (by rebelling), we have turned it around and are not blindly controlled by it. Of course, we must then deal with the consequences of acting contrary to our parents' instructions.

While we have received many messages — some verbal, some non-verbal — there are a few major programs which form the foundation of our lives. It is these major messages which we need to examine. We will be stuck in our programming as long as we are unaware of it. We can change it, but first we need to see it clearly. We must understand which parent gave us which message and how he or she gave it to us.

From our earliest memory, we looked to our mother for love, food and emotional security. She was the first person with whom we came in contact and she plays the most important role in our early development. Her moods become our moods; her thoughts, our thoughts. The bond between mother and child is incredible.

The father's role is to take the child from the emotional security of the home and teach him[1] how to get along in the outer world. The interaction between the parents is the model the child uses in his own relationships for the rest of his life. If the parents are loving and affectionate, his own marriage will be that way. If his father treats his mother poorly, he will do the same to his wife on some level.

We've been told that if we will but live up to the potential indicated in the natal chart, our lives will work well. Why, then, are so many people's lives not working? Are they not living up to the natal potential? Of course they are. That's the trouble. The natal chart shows the messages we received growing up. We continue to live those messages long after the people who gave them to us have passed on. As long as we are attached to our programming, we will not be free to transcend the karmic limitations and implications of our charts. However, astrology has given us an excellent tool for understanding and, hopefully, transcending our programs.

The mother is represented in the natal chart primarily by the Moon, then secondarily by Pluto and/or Saturn. The father is represented primarily by the Sun and secondarily by Saturn. Mother and father are also represented by the fourth and tenth houses, their rulers and planets therein. Aspects to the parental indicators (such as Moon conjunct Venus or Sun square Saturn) give a fuller description of the parent and the message.

The family as a whole can be represented by either the Moon or Saturn, as well as the fourth or tenth house. Grandparents may be indicated by the Moon, Saturn or Pluto, as well as the fourth and tenth houses (if the grandparents assumed the role of parents) and/or the first and seventh houses (the parents' parents). These rules must be applied as each chart directs. While the messages must be synthesized in relation to the entire chart, it is helpful to analyze them step by step.

---

[1]Throughout this book, the word **he** is used generically.

OUR MOTHER'S MESSAGES

THE MOON

While the Moon rules many things, for our purposes we will concentrate on its relation to our mother's messages.

The most important person in our early years is our mother. Because the Moon rules both the mother and the subconscious, her influence reaches us on the deepest levels. It might be argued that since the subconscious is the repository of all past-life experiences, the mother triggers this memory, which is why her influence is so strong.

The mother's main message is to find emotional security. The house in which the Moon is placed natally indicates that area of life in which we hope to find this security. We received this message either directly or indirectly. She told we where we'd find it and we spend the rest of our lives looking for it where she **said** it would be. The sign in which the Moon falls describes the mother, as do the aspects to the Moon. The aspects also tell us if it will be easy or difficult to find the security we seek. Because the Moon is changeable, we find that the promise of emotional security is not always fulfilled. Perhaps this is why we keep returning to the place where it is supposed to be, hoping it will be there this time.

Keep in mind that these messages are not necessarily verbal. We can receive them from her actions as well as her words; by her presence as well as her absence.

The following descriptions are merely guidelines. They should be synthesized with the rest of the chart and not taken out of context. Also, since we're speaking of the subconscious planet, semantics enter the picture. My words may not trigger the same emotional response in all people. Keep this in mind and simply use my explanations as a starting point.

4

The Moon in the Houses

MOON IN 1st: Your mother said to find your emotional security within yourself and on your own. Her influence is very strong, especially if the Moon is close to the Ascendant, in which case you may look like her. She said to take care of yourself first. You may experience mood swings and changes in your personality. You react emotionally and take things personally.

MOON IN 2nd: Your mother gave you a strong emotional need for money. Money may have been important to her. You transferred your security from mother to money. She acts as if she were your possession, and you treat her as such. Because the Moon is changeable, her message may be that your finances — and security — will go up and down, and to try to hang on to them. Notice what you do with your money when you're feeling insecure or unsettled. That will be part of her message.

MOON IN 3rd: Your mother's message was to **think emotionally and to remember not just what happened, but how you felt about what happened**. Your emotional security need may be fulfilled through talking. You are probably quite psychic, but may find it difficult to discern intuition from emotion. The female influence in your early environment was strong. The Moon here can indicate not just Mama, but other female relatives. Travel may help fulfill your security need. Your mother taught you to take your ideas personally, to identify with them emotionally and to think defensively.

MOON IN 4th: The Moon in the fourth leaves no doubt that the mother rules this house, unless the Sun or Saturn is also here, indicating the possibility that both parents should be read into the fourth. The maternal message was to **find your security in your home** — and with your family — and with her. You may find it difficult to be away from home for too long. You can be very protective of your home and family. Your mother's influence will increase as time goes by, whether or not she is living.

MOON IN 5th: Your mother told you to have fun — possibly to have children — but certainly to be creative. She told you to be a

5

child, but indicates that she will be your child (act like one), and for you to treat her like one. This flip-flop of roles can produce a child who acts like a mother to you. You are protective of your children and they are self-protective. (The fifth house is your child's first house.) Your emotional security need is fulfilled through having children and/or through social, sexual or creative outlets.

MOON IN 6th: Your mother said your emotional security need can be fulfilled through service to others, by being needed, and by being busy at all times. You may find that you are protective of, and emotional about, your work. You may be a surrogate mother in your work, nurturing others in some way. You may find security in being healthy — or unhealthy — depending on your mother's message.

MOON IN 7th: Your mother said to get married, that a spouse would provide emotional security. She also said to mother others, which means you'll attract people who are looking for a mother. She wants to be treated as an equal, which is difficult because at some point she can cease being equal and pull rank. Emotional security can elude you because you're looking for a mother in your mate, or at least the mother you'd hoped to have. This placement can be disappointing because, while are are looking for emotional security in another, he is looking for it in himself (our seventh is our mate's first). This means we'll give and he'll take.

MOON IN 8th: Anything in the eighth house needs to be transformed. The best part is that anything in the eighth **will** be transformed in this lifetime. The eighth deals with our hang-ups. The Moon here says there is a very strong emotional attachment to the mother which needs to be analyzed. Your mother taught you to manipulate, in order to control. She may have done this on such subtle levels that you are not aware of all of them. There can be a power play between the two of you. She may have taught you to find your security by helping other people develop their own values, money, or resources. She made a detective out of you, telling you not to trust what's on the surface, but to look beneath the obvious. She may have given you a deep appreciation of the occult as well as a strong

6

psychic ability. She taught you to be in control of your emotions to the point that it may be difficult for you to get in touch with them. She gave you strong attitudes toward sex which can manifest as the need to control sexually. When these messages are transmuted, you will have a deep understanding of universal law.

MOON IN 9th: Your mother said your emotional security need can be fulfilled by living according to your principles, which can be a reflection of hers, as she, too, was a person of principle. Her message was to **keep your mind open to all ideas and live according to God's laws**. She may have encouraged you to travel and pursue higher education. Your philosophy can include self-protectiveness and nurturing, and will change during your lifetime. When upset, you can find peace through communion with God.

MOON IN 10th: Your mother is the tenth-house parent, unless the Sun or Saturn is here, indicating that both parents are involved in this house. Your mother's message was to **be on top**, to be in charge, and to mother the world in your career. If she did this by example, she will dominate any scene in which she plays a part. She told you to be protective of your career and public image. She may have said that there can be changes in your career and to protect what you've got. You identify personally with your position, career, status or public image. You are strongly attached to being a leader.

MOON IN 11th: Your mother taught you to be a friend and she, herself, may want to be your friend. She told you to be different and have unusual friends. She also told you to mother them and look to them for your emotional security. Your emotional security then, can come from being a friend. It's hard for you to be objective about your hopes and wishes. Your friendship circle can change along with your goals. You may try to hang on to friends too long.

MOON IN 12th: Your mother taught you to play a behind-the-scenes role and possibly even to escape through food, drink, sleep, alcohol, drugs, make-believe, etc. Her influence is hard to see clearly since she is posited in the subconscious twelfth.

7

She taught you to fulfill your emotional security need by being alone, possibly by her example. This will cause you to guard your privacy tenaciously. She may have helped you on spiritual levels and in metaphysical study. If the Moon is close to the Ascendant, her influence is like someone standing behind you, peering over your shoulder. You may turn around quickly, hoping to catch a glimpse of her, but she is elusive.

The Moon in the Signs

Your Moon sign describes your mother and her message regarding security.

MOON IN ARIES: Your mother is forthright, direct and impatient. As a result, your moods are quick to rise and need a ready outlet. She, too, is quick on the trigger. Some of your impatience or anger needs to be directed at her instead of others. She taught you to put yourself first. You need a short-term goal with a quick reward. Your emotional security comes through being first, being active, and topping your last attempt.

MOON IN TAURUS: Your mother is patient to the point of stubbornness and can be very set in her ways. She taught you the security of a routine as well as the value of money and possessions. She likes the pleasures of life and may have taught you to relax and take it easy. Your moods are slow to surface, but lie deep. You are emotionally tenacious, which makes it hard to forgive or forget. Your emotional security need is fulfilled through money, a routine and the basics in life.

MOON IN GEMINI: Your mother can be two people in one, each side keeping you guessing. She can be nervous and high strung, and there's a good chance she's talkative. You probably are, too. You both get bored easily and need mental stimulation. Keeping your hands busy is good therapy. Your emotional security need is fulfilled through communication. Humor is an outlet.

MOON IN CANCER: Your mother is nurturing and emotionally tenacious, able to play on your emotions. You are protective and nurturing as well, with a strong attachment to home and family.

Both you and your mother are extremely sensitive, have strong mood swings and tend to take things personally. Your home and family provide your emotional security and you find it hard to let go of them.

MOON IN LEO: Your mother is dramatic, though not necessarily showy. She can pitch a fit for shock value, though, should the need arise. She is creative, loves to have fun and does well with children. All this applies to you as well. She taught you to be a prince (or princess), but will never relinquish her role as queen. She will dominate either obviously or subtly. Your security needs can be fulfilled through being creative and, possibly, through being in the limelight.

MOON IN VIRGO: Your mother tends to worry about the small details of life. She passed this along to you. She is a perfectionist. This comes from feelings of **not** being perfect and, therefore, needing to correct the flaw. She taught you to comprehend, but you may need to learn to understand as well. Health, either good or bad, may be one of her interests. You tend to analyze your moods. Remember that they cannot be put on a computer card. Security comes through perfection and service.

MOON IN LIBRA: Your mother wants peace at any price — even if it means war. She can be charming, but noncommital. Partnership is important to her and she gave you the message to get married or, at least, find a partner. Your emotions, rather than being balanced as the scales imply, tend to swing from one extreme to the other. Security comes through partnership and sharing with others.

MOON IN SCORPIO: Your mother is deep, intense and controlled. She understands instinctively how to manipualte and control, and passed this along to you. The need to be in control at all times, in all situations, is paramount and gives you security. There can be a power play between you and your mother. Each of you needs to learn to forgive. This will help you forget.

MOON IN SAGITTARIUS: Your mother has a great need for freedom and is probably quite philosophical about life. She may tend to exaggerate, but tries to be honest at all times. She taught

9

you to expand your horizons, open your mind to new thoughts, and travel as much as possible. Your emotions tend to be exaggerated, whether up or down, though they are not as intense as the Scorpio Moon's emotions. Your emotional security comes through freedom.

MOON IN CAPRICORN: Your mother takes life seriously and feels a strong sense of responsibility toward home and family, which she passed along to you. She wants to be an authority figure and be respected for following through on her responsibilities. When she gets depressed, she builds a wall around herself for protection. This can make her cold and distant. You may find yourself doing the same thing. You have such a strong sense of responsibility that you find it hard to enjoy yourself. Security comes through being an authority figure. This gives you power.

MOON IN AQUARIUS: Your mother is certainly unusual and may feel she was born before her time. She taught you to be your own person, but you may feel caught between two worlds. You may be torn between doing what you want to do versus doing what you feel you ought to do. At times she can be very traditional, even rigid. Then, at other times, she can let it rip. Eclectic describes her well. Since Aquarius-type people are concerned about the welfare of the group, if the group is happy, they are happy. Herein lies their security. You may ask yourself once a week, "Am I crazy or is the world crazy?" This is because, while you like people, you don't necessarily need them. Others don't understand this and make you feel there's something wrong with you. There isn't; you're fine.

MOON IN PISCES: Your mother tends to be either a dreamy romantic or an escapist. She taught you to either turn the other cheek, knowing it's the nature of love to forgive, or she taught you to be a martyr. Either she chooses not to see negativity around her, preferring to look at the beauty of life, or she cannot see it because her rose-colored glasses have been on too long. There's an element of make-believe about her which may be her emotional security. You both need a cause to live for, a dream about which to build your life. This is a beautiful, spiritual placement for the Moon, but makes it hard to do laundry or to drive a car.

Aspects to the Moon

The aspects the Moon makes in our natal chart tell us not only about our mother and her messages, but about ourselves and our relationship with her.

MOON-SUN-POSITIVE: At the time of your birth, your parents were in harmony, indicating that the male and female qualities are balanced within you. Your parents' positive relationship gave you good role models, enabling you to have fulfilling interpersonal relationships. You get along well with both men and women.

MOON-SUN-NEGATIVE: Conflict between your parents at the time of your birth created a pattern of difficulty in your interpersonal relationships. You are not programmed to get along with others or for things to flow smoothly. This can affect your health.

MOON-MERCURY-POSITIVE: Your mother is able to express herself clearly, and there is good communication between the two of you. This extends to communication with all women and the public in general. There is harmony between your conscious and subconscious minds giving you the ability to articulate your thoughts well.

MOON-MERCURY-NEGATIVE: There can be confusion between you and your mother, as you are communicating on two different levels. Your conscious and subconscious minds are at odds with each other, which can produce nervousness, confusion and the inability to clearly express your thoughts. You may find it tiring to talk to your mother, as you have to explain things more than once. This carries over into conversation with others, so that communication in general may be confused and unsettling.

11

MOON-VENUS-POSITIVE: Your mother is loving and giving and there is a definite bond of love between the two of you. You, in turn, are loving and giving and attract fulfilling relationships and friends who care about you.

MOON-VENUS-NEGATIVE: Your mother does not really know how to show love and may give you things instead of love. This creates the concept of compensation: **if you don't feel loved, you'll eat, spend money or indulge yourself in some way**. This aspect can manifest as laziness in both you and your mother. You can attract self-indulgent, even lazy females to you.

MOON-MARS-POSITIVE: You and your mother deal well with each other's energies. She taught you to channel your energies positively without wasting them. You can get things done quickly and easily. You have a good rapport with both men and women. You function well in competitive situations.

MOON-MARS-NEGATIVE: There is a conflict between you and your mother. You hold much anger, hostility or unresolved resentment toward her. Neither of you can forgive the past. This problem can carry over into your interpersonal relationships. It can make you competitive. Unfortunately, your emotions are not under control which can keep you from winning. There can be difficulty controlling or channeling sexual energy as well. There is a strong need to get back at people for past hurts.

MOON-JUPITER-POSITIVE: You and your mother are friends and enjoy each other's company. As a result, you have many friends and are popular. You are generous and philosophical.

MOON-JUPITER-NEGATIVE: Like the negative aspects between the Moon and Venus, this aspect tends toward overindulgence and exaggeration. Your mother buys love and compensates for lack of it. You tend to exaggerate your moods and attract people who overdo. You may overwhelm people by coming on larger-than-life.

MOON-SATURN-POSITIVE: You respect your mother and older people in general. Your mother is strong and channels her emotions constructively. You're both willing to do whatever is necessary. She's got a good rapport with her family. She imbued you with a strong sense of responsibility and leadership, as well as the ability to get along with authority figures.

MOON-SATURN-NEGATIVE: Your mother is moody and depressed and gave you the message that you're not supposed to be happy — you're supposed to be responsible. It's hard for either of you to have fun — life holds too much responsibility. There can be walls up between you and your mother as well as between your mother and her family. You are afraid of the responsibility and emotional commitment required in a close relationship. This can make you cold, distant and unaffectionate. Lack of love can depress you, which can lead to self-pity.

MOON-URANUS-POSITIVE: Your mother is unique and gave you the freedom to be yourself. Your intuition is keen and your physic bond with her is strong. You attract fascinating females.

MOON-URANUS-NEGATIVE: Your mother is unpredictable and you never know what to expect of her. She taught you to rebel. You both want freedom. You attract self-willed, unpredictable females. Relationships with women can end suddenly and unexpectedly.

MOON-NEPTUNE-POSITIVE: There is a natural spiritual attunement between you and your mother. She gave you the desire to serve unselfishly. She also gave you a love of music, art and the aesthetics, as well as an appreciation of the metaphysics. You both have creative and artistic potential. You feel she is something special. You, in turn, may have a mystical quality about you that attracts people.

MOON-NEPTUNE-NEGATIVE: You do not see your mother clearly. Either she is so wonderful that you feel you'll never live up to her example, or she copped out, leaving you to create your own maternal concept. There is definitely wishful thinking in connection with your mother. She may have avoided reality through drugs, alcohol, food, sleep, etc. Guilt needs to be examined;also martyrdom.You are vulnerable to women who deceive you and must avoid ignoring reality.

MOON-PLUTO-POSITIVE: There is a good psychic bond between you and your mother. You understand each other's feelings. You are a very magnetic person and channel your emotions well. Your psychic ability is strong. You are nurturing without being smothering.

MOON-PLUTO-NEGATIVE: There is a strong power play between you and your mother based on her need to control you and your need to defend yourself. You may be dependent on her and resent the dependency, since that is what holds you prisoner. The need on both your parts to retaliate keeps you hooked into this power play. You find it hard to trust women and can attract jealousy from them. You take things personally and cannot forgive past hurts. This makes you vindictive. You can locate someone else's jugular with uncanny accuracy. You are possessive of those you love and expect their unfailing loyalty. You need to examine your mother's message about sex, especially if you play power or sex games. You tend to attract people with unresolved maternal problems.

MOON-NODES-POSITIVE: Your intuition and emotions are well-balanced and help you learn the lessons your mother is here to teach you. The good rapport you had with women in past lives helps in this one.

MOON-NODES-NEGATIVE: Poor rapport with your mother and women in past lives hinders your relationships with them in this one. The tendency to emotionally hang on to the past prevents success.

PLUTO

Pluto is also part of our mother's message, as well as an indicator of grandparents, particularly the grandmother. Pluto represents total change, control, and transmutation. Pluto deals with all the mysteries of life: life itself, where it originates, where it goes from this plane. It deals with the oedipal concept of mother, which brings in the concept of sex. Pluto and the aspects it makes in our chart tell us much about our attitudes toward sex. Pluto is all or nothing. We may go down in flames, but it won't be for lack of fight.

For our purposes, Pluto's house placement indicates where (which area of life) there will be a power play with the mother — in which area she will try to dominate and control. This is where there we will reverse roles with her, where we will insist on being in control. We control because we don't trust. We don't trust the people who rule the house in which Pluto falls.

While I will be referring to Pluto as the mother, you may substitute the word **grandmother** if and where it is applicable.

Pluto in the Houses

PLUTO IN 1st: Your mother tries to dominate you and control your personality. As a result, you are even more determined to maintain control over yourself. You may not show the emotions you feel in an attempt to maintain control. This is not necessarily done on a conscious level. As time goes by, you essentially become your own authority figure.

PLUTO IN 2nd: You have a great need to control your money and possessions as well as your desire nature. Your mother taught you to **hang on to things**. Your values will undergo a total change and you will be free of your maternal message regarding money and values. Your mother taught you to control with money and make it your tool, but it could wind up controlling you. If she controlled the money, you and she could reverse roles.

PLUTO IN 3rd: There was a reversal of roles between you and your mother when you were a child — unless Pluto is retrograde — in which case, it occurred later. A grandparent may have had a strong influence in your early environment. Your thinking is controlled and you think in terms of how to control each situation. You want to understand the workings of your mind so that you control it, rather than it controlling you. Your thinking, while dominated by your mother, will undergo a total change in this lifetime, enabling you to be free.

15

PLUTO IN 4th: There can be a reversal of roles between you and your mother during the second half of life. At this time you will assume the role of controlling parent. Your mother's control over the family is enormous — even if she is no longer living. Your own emotional security need can be fulfilled by being in control of your home and family. Your mother or grandmother rules the fourth if Pluto is here, unless the Sun or Saturn is also here, in which case the father and/or grandfather may be involved as well. You don't really trust your mother.

PLUTO IN 5th: Your mother may attempt to control your children and, in so doing, control you through them. There can be a total reversal of roles between you and your mother — she can control you by acting like your child. As a result of this role model, you and your oldest child can reverse roles, with you controlling your child by acting like the child. Your child will attempt to control himself in an attempt to be free of your domination. You may try to dominate sexually by withholding. This, however, can deprive you of enjoyment.

PLUTO IN 6th: Your mother's attempt to control your work makes you determined to be in control. There may be something about your work which was not invented or discovered at the time of your birth. There can be a total change in your work at some point in your life. The need to maintain constant control at work and/or the inability to forgive those who would attempt to control you in this area can affect your health, especially the elimination or sexual areas. When we hang on and control, there is an improper flow. This causes toxins to build up in the system. The answer is forgiveness of those who have hurt you, which will free you of vindication.

PLUTO IN 7th: Your mate attempts to control you and, on a subconscious level pushes the **mama button**, thus creating a power play in the marriage. This can lead to divorce if the principles of power, control and domination are not worked out. You and your spouse will each feel the other's control. This results in the need to defend the self and overthrow the other. Your mother insists on being treated as an equal. She controls your marriage through her spoken or unspoken messages. (It was she who gave you the **control your spouse** message in the

16

first place.) Since you are reversing roles with your mother in your marriage, your mate will see you as his mother and react in kind (remember that your seventh is his first).

PLUTO IN 8th: The need for power, control and dominance is extremely strong. You are extremely intense in your need to be in control of yourself. You live to be in control. You will not permit yourself to make a mistake. You have a strong need to vindicate yourself, but won't waste your energy on small skirmishes. With you it's all or nothing, so when you wage war it is nuclear in scope. You are willing to fight to the death. Your sexual drives need to be understood and transmuted, or they will control you. Your interest in all the secrets of life makes you an excellent researcher. Your psychic powers are very strong, but must be used constructively. It is important that you understand the control your mother has over you, for she is the one who gave you all these messages.

PLUTO IN 9th: Your mother gave you the message that **your philosophy should include, or even be built around, the concept of control**. You can justify control by rationalizing that **there's a principle involved**. Your attitude toward God may be that you are controlled and want, therefore, to be in control of yourself. Your philosophy of life and attitude toward God, as given to you by your mother, can undergo a total change in this lifetime.

PLUTO IN 10th: Your mother's message was to **be in control in your career** and be a powerful authority figure. She tries to dominate your public image either by riding your coattails or competing with you for the limelight. You do not trust her. You want to dethrone her and assume leadership yourself. You probably will. She is the out-front parent and rules the tenth house, unless Pluto describes your grandmother, or unless the Sun or Saturn are here, indicating the father's influence as well. There can be a total change in your career at some point in your life. You have a magnetic, compelling public image.

PLUTO IN 11th: Your mother's message was to **be a friend**, but to control any group in which you participate. She gave you the message that your friends control you. This makes you mistrust them. She can control your hopes and wishes and possibly your friendship circle. She wants to be your friend, but can control you by switching from friend to mother. Your friends see you as powerful, but manipulative.

PLUTO IN 12th: Your mother's message is hard to see because it is hidden in the subconscious twelfth. It is from this vantage point that she controls you. You may be aware, though not entirely, of this control. You are not sure why, but there is a part of you that does not completely trust her. She taught you to **control from behind-the-scenes**. Introspection and self-analysis are important in order to see her messages.

Pluto in the Signs

Since Pluto is one of our generational planets, its sign placement is the same for millions of people. It deals with group karma and the major lessons each generation has to learn. It affects people less on a personal level and more on a mass level. Since our purpose here is to look at the personal messages, I will touch lightly on Pluto in the signs.

PLUTO IN CANCER: Changed our attitudes about self-protection, home and family. We broke free from many of the hang-ups we had about emotional security.

PLUTO IN LEO: Changed our attitudes about power and authority.

PLUTO IN VIRGO: Gave us a different attitude about work and health.

PLUTO IN SCORPIO: Will teach us lessons about control and the transmutation of power, especially nuclear power.

Aspects to Pluto

Pluto's aspects in our natal chart tell us about our mother and our relationship with each other:

PLUTO-SUN-POSITIVE: Good psychic bonds between your parents at the time of your birth gave you positive role models. They taught you to assume command without abusing power. They taught you to get along with those in authority as well as those who follow your lead. You can be a pioneer. You are magnetic and psychic and get along well with both men and women.

PLUTO-SUN-NEGATIVE: At the time of your birth your parents were involved in a power play. There was a lack of trust between them. They could not forgive and forget. This led to resentment and vindication on the part of both parents and set the tone for your own interpersonal relationships. You are manipulative and controlling and find it hard to trust others. You do not forget past hurts. You want to dominate and lead, and resent those who do.

PLUTO-MOON-POSITIVE: There is a strong psychic bond between you and your mother. She may have had a similar bond with her mother. You find it easy to understand and get along with women. Your feelings for your home and family are strong, yet positive. You are a magnetic person with a strong intuition. There is a natural mothering quality about you that does not smother or possess.

PLUTO-MOON-NEGATIVE: There is a strong power play between you and your mother based on her need to control you and your need to defend yourself. You may be dependent on her and resent the dependency, since that is what holds you prisoner. You find it hard to trust women, and can attract jealousy from them. You take things personally and find it hard to forgive past hurts. This makes you vindictive. You can locate someone else's jugular with uncanny accuracy. You are possessive of those you love and expect their unfailing loyalty. You need to look at your mother's message regarding sex, especially if you tend to play power or sex games. You tend to attract people with unresolved maternal problems.

PLUTO-MERCURY-POSITIVE: You and your mother are able to communicate without speaking, the psychic bond between you is so strong. This carries over into your conversations with others. You can spot truth from falsehood and are a natural detective. Your intuition is so much a part of you that you do not see it as unusual.

PLUTO-MERCURY-NEGATIVE: It may be hard to communicate with your mother because you cannot trust her not to entrap you with your own words. This can extend to others, making you suspicious and mistrustful. Your mind is quick and deep, but negative psychic impressions can block the flow. You may pick up more negative vibes than positive. You may have a hope-for-the-best-but-expect-the-worst approach to life.

PLUTO-VENUS-POSITIVE: You feel deeply loved by your mother and this makes you a loving person in return. Your mother gave you positive messages regarding love and sex, which permits you to enjoy both. You are creative and can enjoy the good things in life without going overboard.

PLUTO-VENUS-NEGATIVE: Your mother's messages regarding love and sex are at odds with each other, giving you conflicting messages about both. Your desire nature is strong, but can be suppressed. Women may have been given the message that **nice girls don't**. While you love your mother, there can be sexual competition with her if you are a woman, and confused or suppressed desire for her if you are a man. This can affect your relationships with women, creating the need to control and dominate sexually in order to possess.

PLUTO-MARS-POSITIVE: Your mother had a good rapport with men and passed this along to you. You have lots of energy when you need it and can direct it positively. Your sex drive is well-channeled and you are able to compete on a positive level with others. Your mother gave you the freedom to assert yourself.

PLUTO-MARS-NEGATIVE: You may feel strong, yet suppressed resentment at the control your mother exerts over you and an equally strong need to retaliate. The tendency toward vindication is strong, as is the need to conquer. Your competitive side is strong and can get out of hand, which can force you into precipitous action. Past hurts are hard to forget. They build up and create the competition or vengeance situation. The underlying feeling of this aspect is **kill or be killed**. Your sex drives are strong and can control you.

PLUTO-JUPITER-POSITIVE: You and your mother are good friends. You may share similar philosophies or, if you don't at least you give each other the space to have your own opinions. She taught you to be optimistic, generous and friendly. As a result, you are well-liked. You have a natural understanding of cosmic law that gives you peace.

PLUTO-JUPITER-NEGATIVE: Jupiter expands whatever it touches, so your mother's control is very strong. Equally strong is your need to be free. This need for freedom is really a desire to be in control so as not to be controlled. Your mother taught you to exaggerate. This can send you to extremes. You may tend to be vindictive and justify it under the heading of **standing on principle**. Your strong sexual drives can be channeled into causes and philosophies.

PLUTO-SATURN-POSITIVE: The good rapport between your parents and grandparents gave you respect for authority figures and the ability to get along well with them. You have a good sense of responsibility. You don't go overboard in the use of power. You respect it. You understand how to lead and what must be done without having to use manipulation. You can both delegate authority and follow instruction. Your psychic energies are well-channeled.

PLUTO-SATURN-NEGATIVE: The authority figures in your life did not get along. They resented and rebelled against authority while exercising their own authority over you. This double message causes you to lock horns with authority figures now. You resent having to obey someone just because he's in authority. Your fear of being controlled by those in power makes you rebel. Actually, you want to be the authority figure. Once in power, though, you're afraid of being undermined. In order to protect yourself, you will act like the authority figures you resented as a child.

PLUTO-URANUS-POSITIVE: Your mother's message was to be creative, be your own person. Her positive reinforcement of your intuitive and creative abilities encouraged you to express yourself inventively.

PLUTO-URANUS-NEGATIVE: You will rebel against any attempts to restrict your free will. This message was given to you by your mother. Your psychic ability is active, but you are suspicious. This can cloud your perception. You can go to extremes at times in your need for independence.

PLUTO-NEPTUNE-POSITIVE: There is a positive psychic bond between you and your mother. Your spiritual side is active, and you have vision and insight.

PLUTO-NEPTUNE-NEGATIVE: While you may sense your mother's control, it is hard to see it clearly. She may control you indirectly. This can lead to rebellious escapes: drugs, alcohol, etc.

PLUTO-NODES-POSITIVE: You have a natural understanding of the psychic forces and will use them positively. There is a deep psychic bond between you and your mother. She will be an important teacher to you.

PLUTO-NODES-NEGATIVE: The misuse of psychic energies in past lives can lead you to use manipulation and control in order to get your way. This will backfire. The inability to trust your mother and the fear of being controlled (from past lives) makes it difficult for you to trust (in this one).

OUR FATHER'S MESSAGES

The father's role is that of leading us from the security of the home and teaching us how to act in society. He helps us form our public image, the face we want the world to see. He teaches us to be our own person.

THE SUN

As such, the Sun represents the father. (While the Sun represents many things, for our purposes we will look at it in terms of our father's message to us.) Keep in mind that he gave us these messages by his presence or absence, verbally or nonverbally.

The Sun in the Houses

SUN IN 1st: Your father taught you to put yourself first and express your power, authority and individuality. Unfortunately, his influence can be so strong that he can actually inhibit you. If the Sun is close to the Ascendant, his influence is greater, and you may look like him. While you will act like him, you will feel that you are your own authority figure. This can be unsettling to your father, who may either turn to you as his authority figure or compete with you. This is because our fathers want us to succeed, but their egos don't want their children to surpass them. You need to watch the tendency to be self-centered and assume that everyone else's world revolves around you.

SUN IN 2nd: Your father's message was **to make money**, and he taught you how, either by his presence or absence. He taught you to be proud of your possessions and to be creative with money. His message was that **money gives authority and power**. This can make money the center of your life. Your father may have given you the message that he, too, is one of your possessions.

SUN IN 3rd: Your father's message was that **when he spoke you were to listen**. He taught you that your ideas are important. As a result your ego can be wrapped up in your ideas and you may be quite attached to them. There is a strong male influence in your early environment. Your father molded your thinking and you may tend to think a lot like him, which means you think in terms of power and authority. Your ideas are creative, but you want others to listen to them and agree with them.

SUN IN 4th: The fourth house is your father rather than your mother, unless the Moon or Pluto is also posited here. You look to your father to fulfill your emotional security needs. His message was that **your home and family should be the center of your life**. Your ego can be wrapped up in providing security for your family. By his presence or absence, he gave you the message that **you are to be the king in your home**. His messages will get stronger as time goes by. The second half of life should be more fulfilling for you than the first.

SUN IN 5th: Your father taught you to be creative and/or to have fun and/or to be a kid. You may find, as time goes by, that you reverse roles with your father, as his underlying message is that he's the kid. He taught you to be dramatic in whatever you do and possibly to take a chance. He also taught you to be proud of anything you create, including children. Your ego can be involved in your creations, though, giving you too much pride.

SUN IN 6th: The center of your life is your work and you have to be busy at all times. Your father taught you to take pride in what you do, but not to be above tending to the small details. He was either proud of his health — or lack of it — and passed this along to you.

SUN IN 7th: You are looking for your father in your partner, be it business or personal. His message was to **put other people first**, to treat them as equals — particularly himself. As a result, you will treat authority figures as your equals. The center of your life is your partner, which is fortunate, because the center of your partner's life is himself (your seventh is your partner's first). You are programmed to give, which means you will attract people who will take. You are proud of your partner — and he is proud of himself.

SUN IN 8th: Your father's message was to **be secretive and hold your cards close to your chest**. He also gave you the message to **help other people develop their own resources**. He was a detective of sorts, and taught you to look beyond the obvious. He also taught you self-control. Your attitude toward your father must undergo a change so that you can grow. He taught you to compensate for insecurities by manipulating, controlling, and putting others on the defensive. He hid a great deal of himself and you do the same. Unfortunately, you can hide from yourself as well as others. It is therefore, important to ask yourself why you do the things you do. Until you understand your real motivation, you will not be in control of yourself.

SUN IN 9th: You are proud of your philosophy and try to live according to your principles. Your father played a big part in molding your philosophy of life as well as your attitude toward God. Your father may have traveled a good bit, and encouraged you to expand your horizons, possibly through education. As a result you try to see the total picture, not just bits and pieces.

SUN IN 10th: Unless the Moon and/or Pluto are here, this house is your father. His message was to **be the leader**, be the boss, be on top. He taught you to **be proud of your career**. He may have set the example. This makes it hard for him to take a back seat to you should you begin to surpass him. You will be given power, responsibility and authority in this lifetime. You can eaily be in the limelight.

SUN IN 11th: Your father taught you to be a friend, but to **be an authority figure to your friends**. You want to lead any group to which you belong. Your father may want to be your friend, but will still be your authority figure. That can be a difficult fence to straddle. Your father taught you to be proud of your friends — and to have important, influential friends.

SUN IN 12th: Your father taught you to **pull back and be the power-behind-the-scenes**. He taught you to guard your privacy. He may have been an absentee father and/or stayed to himself a lot. You may find it easy to escape and avoid reality. Watch out for martydom. Since the Sun is hidden in the twelfth, it is hard for you to see your father clearly.

The Sun in the Signs

Traditionally, we look at Sun signs to tell us about ourselves. In this case, we are going to examine the Sun sign to get a clearer picture of what our father was like. Since it's hard to get our egos out of the way, this may take a little practice.

SUN IN ARIES: Your father is direct and wants his ego needs satisfied **now**. He gave you the same message. He can be impatient and is always looking for a fire to put out. He taught you to be **aggressive, active.**

SUN IN TAURUS: Your father is practical, stubborn and loves the basics in life. He taught you to **appreciate money** and what it can buy. He may have taught you to relax and, even to be lazy.

SUN IN GEMINI: Your father taught you to think and **use your brain**. While he may not have been a talker, he was certainly an idea man.

SUN IN CANCER: Your father taught you to protect yourself, your home and your family. He taught you to **take care of your own security needs**. He may have been moody. He taught you to either give or receive nurturing.

SUN IN LEO: Your father taught you to be dramatic and creative. He may have taught you to have fun. His attitude is: life is a game — play it to the hilt.

26

SUN IN VIRGO: Your father taught you that **perfection is its own reward**. He taught you to work and worry — and pay attention to the details.

SUN IN LIBRA: Your father taught you to deal in partnership. He taught you charm and diplomacy. He may have gone from one extreme to the other. Hopefully, this taught you moderation.

SUN IN SCORPIO: Your father taught you to **be a private, possibly manipulative person**, but certainly one who is in control of himself. His message was not to trust what you see or hear, but to look below the surface to see what's really going on.

SUN IN SAGITTARIUS: Your father gave you a philosophical approach to life. He taught you to **be generous and outgoing** — and to justify whatever you do.

SUN IN CAPRICORN: Your father taught you the value of the dollar and the importance of power. He taught you to **assume responsibility** and be mature.

SUN IN AQUARIUS: Your father taught you to **be your own person**. He gave you a respect for the world as a whole and taught you to trust each person with dignity. He said to put the welfare of the group before personal needs.

SUN IN PISCES: Your father taught you to **be creative** as well as idealistic. He gave you a discontent with what is. He taught you to either serve or escape.

Aspects to the Sun

The Sun's natal aspects tell us a lot about our fathers and their messages, as well as a lot about ourselves.

SUN-MOON-POSITIVE: At the time of your birth, your parents were in harmony, indicating that the male and female qualities are balanced within you. Your parents' positive relationship gave you good role models, enabling you to have fulfilling interpersonal relationships. You get along well with men and women.

27

SUN-MOON-NEGATIVE: Difficulties your father has in interrelating are part of your ego pattern. You are programmed to have difficulties in interpersonal relationships because of difficulties between your parents at the time of your birth. This can affect your health.

SUN-MERCURY: Your father has a one-track mind, making it hard for
(closer than 10°) him to concentrate on more than one thing at a time. The same applies to you. You can only discuss what interests **you**. He does not give you enough space to be objective about him.

SUN-MERCURY: Your father taught you to stand back from situations
(more than 10° apart) and people in order to see them objectively. This applies to him as well. You are able to converse with others without constantly bringing the conversation back to yourself and your opinions.

SUN-VENUS-POSITIVE: Your father is warm and loving. You feel secure in his love. You, too, are warm and loving. People like you. You have an appreciation of beauty and may be artistically talented.

SUN-VENUS-NEGATIVE: (This can only occur by mutual reception.) Your father finds it hard to express his love and compensates by giving you things instead of love. This gives you the message that love equals compensation (money, food, clothes, etc.). You need to curb the tendency to overdo and overindulge.

SUN-MARS-POSITIVE: Your father is direct and assertive, yet channels his energies well. He taught you to do the same. Your sex drive is well-directed and you enjoy a certain amount of competition. While you want to win, you are a good sport. You deal well with men. You have lots of energy and vitality.

SUN-MARS-NEGATIVE: Competition between you and your father, as well as resentment at him is reflected in your combative nature. You are argumentative and ready for a fight. Your attitude is, **Anything you can do, I can do better**. This can manifest as sexual competition, as your sex drive is strong

28

and needs an outlet. Your father wants his way and so do you. You want to win, but if your father always wins, you're just setting yourself up to be defeated and continue the resentment.

SUN-JUPITER-POSITIVE: Your father is friendly, outgoing and generous. He has lots of friends and is well-liked. He is philosophical and sees things optimistically. He passed all this along to you.

SUN-JUPITER-NEGATIVE: Your father is self-indulgent and tends to exaggerate. He can make promises and not deliver. This leads to compensation. He proves his love by giving you things. You will do the same things.

SUN-SATURN-POSITIVE: Your father is strong and dignified. You respect him and all authority figures. They, in turn, respect you. You have an old head on young shoulders. Your father taught you to assume responsibilities and not consider them a burden. You get along well with older men.

SUN-SATURN-NEGATIVE: Your father is cold, aloof and distant. He taught you to build a wall around yourself, which keeps others from getting close. He wants your respect rather than your love. You may show him respect out of fear of what he will do if you don't. He himself fears and resents authority figures. You feel that way about him and, as a result, other authority figures. You want to be an authority figure in order to show him. He cannot show love. You, too, have difficulty in this area.

SUN-URANUS-POSITIVE: Your father is inventive, intuitive and encouraged you to be your own person. He has a strong humanitarian side that puts the welfare of the group first. He is unique and is comfortable with this. He has passed this along to you.

SUN-URANUS-NEGATIVE: Your father is self-willed, rebellious and unpredictable. So are you. You attract this type of male to you. It is hard to stay with one person or situation for too long. Your need for freedom is too strong.

SUN-NEPTUNE-POSITIVE: Your father taught you spirituality and self-lessness. He is kind and willing to serve. You see only the best in people because you see only the best in him — and he taught you to see only the best in yourself. He is an inspiration to you. This is the type of male you will attract.

SUN-NEPTUNE-NEGATIVE: Your concept of your father is not clear, either because you have him on such a high pedestal that he is out of sight, or because he copped out and did not give a substantial role model. He is either wonderful or not much at all. In either case, the issue is clouded. You tend to see yourself the same way: either you are wonderful or just no good. You can be irresponsible and unreliable and attract that type of male to you. The men in your life are irresponsible and disappoint you. You have a tendency to cop out, avoid reality, and indulge in self-pity and martyrdom. You can be manipulated by guilt.

SUN-PLUTO-POSITIVE: Good psychic bonds between your parents at the time of your birth gave you positive role models. They taught you to assume command without abusing power. They taught you to get along with those in authority as well as those who follow your lead. You can be a pioneer. You are magnetic and psychic.

SUN-PLUTO-NEGATIVE: At the time of your birth, your parents were involved in a power play. There was a lack of trust between them. They could not forgive and forget. This led to resentment and vindication, and set the tone for your own inter-personal relationships. You are manipulative and controlling and find it hard to trust others. You attract this type of person to you. You do not forget past hurts. You want to dominate and lead, and resent those who do.

SUN-NODES-POSITIVE: You have a good rapport with your father and men in general as a result of same in past lives. You can attain power and authority in this life.

SUN-NODES-NEGATIVE: You can have difficulties in your relationships with men due to too strong an ego. There can be losses involved with power and authority in this lifetime.

MESSAGES FROM AUTHORITY FIGURES

SATURN

As a child, Saturn is our disciplinarian; as an adult, our teacher. Saturn is reality and often, restriction. In the natal chart, it can represent our father, grandparents, family, or even our mother — anyone who imposes a restrictive influence on our life and tries to teach us reality through discipline. Substitute the word, **father, grandparents**, etc., whichever applies, for **authority figures.**

Saturn in the Houses

SATURN IN 1st: The authority figures in your life taught you to assume responsibility early, making you seem older than your years. The message was, **be a big boy/girl**. You are supposed to assume the responsibility for your family. This gives you a serious attitude and can cause you to build a wall around yourself. You modeled your behavior after the authority figures in your life. This caused you to become distant, authoritative and, possibly, unapproachable. While you may at first have been reluctant to assume responsiblity, you felt it was expected of you. Saturn in the first often indicates the oldest or the only child.

SATURN IN 2nd: The authority figures in your life gave you a fear of not having enough money. Your fear can bring this into being.

31

Real estate and other Saturn-ruled occupations can offset this fear and use the energy positively. Your authority figures told you that money equals power and may have suggested a conservative approach to earning it.

SATURN IN 3rd: Once again, this is the placement of the oldest or only child. The message from authority figures was to think like an adult, which means taking life seriously. There was strong discipline in your early environment, and the possibility that grandparents played an important role. You may feel that you look at things realistically. Others might say that you see things negatively. This is a hope-for-the-best-but-expect-the-worst placement.

SATURN IN 4th: You regard this parent as an authority figure. Grandparents can play an important role in your home life. You feel responsible for your family's security. This can make you feel restricted. Your family is run by an authority figure. The fourth-house parent is very disciplined, traditional and can instill fear in you. You may feel responsible for this parent's security and, on some level, responsible for any unhappiness he/she experiences.

SATURN IN 5th: The authority figures in your life gave you the message that **you should be afraid of having too much fun**. As a result, you may find it hard to enjoy yourself, to loosen up. This may manifest as an inability to express yourself. It can also inhibit your sexual expression. Your children are a responsibility, although the oldest is quite mature for his age. Creative projects may fall short of the mark since you are not supposed to be creative.

SATURN IN 6th: The authority figures in your life said that you need to work hard and be in a responsible position. This can make you the authority figure at work. While you may be afraid of responsibility being dumped on you, you accept it, since it gives you a measure of power. Health matters relating to restriction, resistance and calcification indicate an unbending attitude.

SATURN IN 7th: The authority figures in your life gave you the message that **partnership involves responsibility and restriction**. As a result, you feel held down by your partner. Your authority figures act as if they are your equal, which can be unsettling to you — and you may treat authority figures as your equal, which can be unsettling to them. You attract partners who are cool, distant, stoic, undemonstrative or in some way remind you of an older person. They take themselves seriously.

SATURN IN 8th: You will work through all your fears in this lifetime: fear of the unknown, fear of authority figures, fear of sex, fear of power and authority, fear of being controlled, etc. (You do not necessarily have all of them!) Your authority figures gave you the message that your partner's money can be restricted or insufficient. Their sexual message might have been to manipulate by withholding. This leaves you fearful of what might happen should you not withhold — it makes you feel vulnerable.

SATURN IN 9th: The authority figures in your life may have indicated that God is wrathful and vengeful, and should be feared. Their approach to God was probably a traditionally religious one. Your philosophy involves respect for and fear of power. Your education may have been restricted. You take your principles seriously.

SATURN IN 10th: This parent is the authority figure. There is a strong authoritarian note to your upbringing, with grandparents possibly playing an important role. The tenth-house parent is traditional, strict, unbending, distant and powerful. He instills fear in you, which can manifest as respect, since that is what he wants. You feel it is your responsibility to be a leader, yet you may be fearful of being restricted. You like the status and power it brings, though. As a result of being told to take your career seriously and be in a position of power, you may not like doing menial tasks. You may have a dictatorial attitude toward subordinates. You may be involved in real estate or a family business.

SATURN IN 11th: The authority figures in your life told you to be a friend, but that there were restrictions involved in being one. You may limit your group or friendship activity as a result. When involved with groups or friends, you must be the authority figure. This may make it difficult to be a friend, because friends are supposed to be equals. How can they be equals when you are the authority figure? You may find it easier to be friendly with older people or people you've known for years. Your authority figures may want to be your friends, or they may have told you to select friends from family members.

SATURN IN 12th: The influence of authority figures in your life is difficult for you to see, since it is suppressed. There is a general fear of the unknown, which makes you reluctant to look at them. You may find that you have a constant gnawing doubt about something. The message is to **hold back and stay watchful**. Your authority figures told you to be the power behind-the-scenes. The tendency to feel martyred — as well as guilty — is strong. Use this as a starting point by asking yourself why you feel this way. This will help you see into your twelfth.

Saturn in the Signs

Saturn's sign placement adds another dimension to the description of the authority figures in your life and their messages.

SATURN IN ARIES: The authority figures in your life taught you to **never take a back seat to anyone**, and to insist on doing things your way. You are not afraid of doing what you want, but can be self-centered.

SATURN IN TAURUS: The authority figures in your life taught you to be stubborn. They said money is power, but may have given you the fear of not having enough. This makes you tenacious, but helps you save.

SATURN IN GEMINI: The authority figures in your life tended to see the negative while insisting they were seeing the positive. They labeled this being realistic. They said you could do two things at once, then questioned your ability to do so. It may be difficult to express your ideas completely, possibly because you see both sides of every situation.

SATURN IN CANCER: The authority figure in your life told you to **be responsible for your home and family**. They told you to feel, yet hold your emotions in check. You are sensitive — you just don't show it.

SATURN IN LEO: The authority figures in your life acted like they were born to rule. They passed this along to you. It is hard for a king to show love. Pride gets in the way and builds walls between monarch and subjects.

SATURN IN VIRGO: The authority figures in your life gave you a fear of not being perfect and a concern over small details. The fear of not being needed is another message. You tend to worry, possibly about health.

SATURN IN LIBRA: The authority figures in your life taught you responsibility in relationships. They may have given you the message that relationships involve restriction. This may tend to make you fearful of partnership in general and marriage in particular.

SATURN IN SCORPIO: The authority figures in your life gave you the fear of being controlled by others, which makes you secretive and manipulative. You have a strong need for power.

SATURN IN SAGITTARIUS: The authority figures in your life may have been frustrated because they were not free, yet accepted this philosophically. They taught you to be judicial and balance man's law with God's law.

SATURN IN CAPRICORN: Your authority figures were hard-working, practical and very disciplined. Prestige, status and money were important to them and they taught you to be concerned with appearances. They taught you to go after power.

SATURN IN AQUARIUS: Your authority figures were humanitarians, but still wanted to do things their way. They may have felt frustrated by society. They were set in their ways and sure they were right. They passed this along to you.

SATURN IN PISCES: Fears and doubts clouded the dreams of the authority figures in your life. They may have passed their insecurities along to you which can lead to a defeatist attitude and/or martyrdom.

Aspects to Saturn

Aspects to Saturn tell us a lot about the authority figures in our lives, the limitations they set for us as well as the lessons they taught us.

SUN-SATURN-POSITIVE: The authority figures in your life taught you respect for tradition, family and elders. You are treated with respect because that is what you give others. You are mature and willing to assume your own responsibilities. You have good leadership potential. You may be closer to your father's side of the family.

SUN-SATURN-NEGATIVE: You have a fear of authority figures which can masquerade as respect. You're afraid that if you don't give them the respect they want, they will impose more restrictions on you. They were traditional, rigid and built walls around themselves. You resent authority figures because you want to be one yourself. Yet, responsibility implies a certain amount of restriction to you. You prefer respect to love. Deep emotions make you uncomfortable.

SATURN-MOON-POSITIUE: You feel secure with the authority figures in your life because they made you feel this way. They got along, which taught you to get along with older people. You have a good blend of caring and responsibility without the burden of obligation. You may be closer to your mother's side of the family.

SATURN-MOON-NEGATIVE: Restrictions imposed by the (female) authority figures in your life gave you the message that you are not supposed to be happy. There is an element of moodiness and/or sadness coloring your emotions. You may feel that women and/or family are a restrictive element. You may

36

feel responsible for making your family happy, possibly because you feel responsible, on some level, for their unhappiness. As a result, you cannot be happy while anyone in your family is unhappy. This does not leave you much energy for interpersonal relationships. It is hard for you to get in touch with your emotions. It is easier to suppress them.

SATURN-MERCURY-POSITIVE: The authority figures in your life taught you to think practically, logically and conservatively. You can analyze situations objectively.

SATURN-MERCURY-NEGATIVE: The authority figures in your life have curtailed your thinking. You think you're being realistic when, in fact, you're being negative. The fear that something may go wrong has you looking for it. As a result, you see flaws. This is what the authority figures in your life taught you to do. There is another side to this coin: there are times when the fear of what you might see prevents your looking. You ultimately look because you want to be prepared for the worst.

SATURN-VENUS-POSITIVE: The authority figures in your life gave you a secure feeling of being loved. As a result, you are loyal in love and able to maintain a long-term relationship. You do not take love lightly. When you love, you willingly assume whatever responsibilities are involved in the relationship. You're not looking for wild, exciting love unless Mars or Uranus is involved in this configuration. You are looking for a steady, reliable love.

SATURN-VENUS-NEGATIVE: You never felt loved by the authority figures in your life, so you are not programmed to give or receive love. This means you're not supposed to be happy. As a result, there is always an element of sadness or depression which colors every happy situation. It's almost Pavlovian: if you're happy, you have to be unhappy. The authority figures in your life were unhappy and gave you the message that **love involves hurt, responsibility, unhappiness and/or possibly loss.** Who can blame you for not wanting it? Any time love comes close, you'll sabotage it and push it away. You may have gotten the message that you cannot be happy until your family is, which means your first responsibility is to your family. Since there will always be someone who is unhappy, you may never get around to yourself.

SATURN-MARS-POSITIVE: The authority figures in your life taught you to be brave and strong. You can take direction as well as lead, which gives you a good rapport with anyone in authority. You are disciplined and hard-working. You do not fear leadership and are not too important to take care of the small details of any job. Your energies are well-directed.

SATURN-MARS-NEGATIVE: The authority figures in your life probably gave orders instead of guidance and direction. As a result you both resent and fear them. This can make you fight the establishment, since you feel you could do better. Inhibitions prevent the constructive flow of energies. This can be sexually frustrating. There is a tone of suppressed anger about you.

SATURN-JUPITER-POSITIVE: The authority figures in your life were judicial, fair and taught you to balance what you want to do against what you ought to do. Their philosophy helps you combine God's law with man's law. You're able to see both sides of the picture. You have a wisdom that belies your age. Your message is: **every cloud has a silver lining.**

SATURN-JUPITER-NEGATIVE: You experience conflicts between doing what you want to do and doing what you feel you ought to do. Even when enjoying yourself, you feel limited. This message came to you from the authority figures in your life who would pull you back when you were enjoying yourself too much. They may have set the example by doing the same with themselves. Their concept of God involved fear. This can curb your enthusiasm since the implication is that if you have too much fun, God will punish you — there is a price to pay for all happiness — Karma's waiting just around the corner. In other words: **every silver lining has a cloud.**

SATURN-URANUS-POSITIVE: You are able to break loose, be yourself and still not lose your dignity. This is because the authority figures in your life gave you permission to do so. You are a combination of the traditional and non-traditional and can combine the best of old and new. You can deal with the masses and still remain in charge of yourself. You can put your inventions into practical application.

SATURN-URANUS-NEGATIVE: You are torn between breaking free and assuming your responsibilities. You rebel against being told what to do, and resent any restriction to your freedom. Yet, you feel compelled to go along with the program, even half-heartedly. The authority figures in your life felt trapped between two generations, and you may feel the same way. You can identify with older as well as younger people, traditional and non-traditional groups. You will vacillate between towing the line and breaking free. The authority figures in your life probably rebelled against the authority figures in their lives, yet restricted you. The double message: **rebel, but conform.**

SATURN-NEPTUNE-POSITIVE: The authority figures in your life helped you put your dreams into action by looking at them realistically. You have a certain reverence for authority figures. You can combine mysticism with religion, and bring a practical approach to the metaphysical. You're not afraid to examine your dreams in the light of day.

SATURN-NEPTUNE-NEGATIVE: The authority figures in your life were insecure about their own abilities and taught you to doubt your own. You are afraid to look too closely at your dreams, possibly because your authority figures poked holes in them, or possibly because every time you reached for success they laid a guilt trip on you. No matter. The result is that you are afraid of success and will sabotage it when it comes too close.

SATURN-PLUTO-POSITIVE: The good rapport between the authority figures in your life gave you a respect for your elders and the ability to get along with them. You have a good sense of responsibility. You don't go overboard in the use of power. You respect it. You understand how to lead without having to use manipulation. You can both delegate authority and follow instructions. Your psychic energies are well-channeled.

SATURN-PLUTO-NEGATIVE: The authority figures in your life did not get along. They resented and rebelled against authority in their lives, while exercising their own authority with you. This double message causes you to lock horns with authority figures now. You resent having to obey someone just because he's in authority. Your fear of being controlled by those in power makes you rebel. Actually, you want to be the authority figure. Once in power, though, you're afraid of being undermined. In order to protect yourself, you will act like the authority figures you resented as a child.

SATURN-NODES-POSITIVE: Good rapport with authority figures in past lives makes it easy to get along with them in this one. You will learn the lessons that society has to teach. You can attain power and use it wisely.

SATURN-NODES-NEGATIVE: Your fear of being restricted by authority figures comes from past lives and affects you in this one. Fear can restrict the attainment of power. Power must be handled wisely in this lifetime.

THE FOURTH
AND TENTH HOUSES

The fourth house relates to home, family and our deepest emotional security needs. It describes the parent to whom we looked for the fulfillment of these needs. Traditional astrology gives the mother rulership over this house because she is supposed to be the nurturing parent. Also, because she is, traditionally, the one who stayed at home to care for the family. With the changing times, though, mother often pursues a career, and it is father who provides the emotional security. That is why there are no set rules as to which parent rules which house. Sometimes one parent has to fulfill both roles. Other times the parents reverse roles. Each chart must be analyzed individually in this regard.

The tenth house rules our career, our public image and the authority figure(s) in our life. It is our father who teaches us how to get along in the world outside the home. As such, the tenth house traditionally relates to him. (Except, of course, when it doesn't!) Our mother teaches us love; our father teaches us responsibility.

The relationship between the fourth and tenth is important because our home and family, and the security they give us, determine how we will do outside the home. If we don't get what we need from one parent, we may turn to the other, who may be just as incapable as the first of giving us what we need. Lack of emotional security in the home can lead to compensation in the career. The career, then, becomes a parent replacement. Notice how many people drive themselves in an effort to achieve success in their careers. Since the tenth rules both the career and the tenth house parent, the connection becomes clear.

The signs on the cusps of the fourth and tenth houses add another dimension to understanding our parents. When trying to determine which house is which parent, it is helpful to exaggerate the descriptions enough to allow yourself to be able to make a distinction between the two.

41

Signs on the Fourth and Tenth

ARIES ON 4th: This parent puts himself/herself first. He/she is impatient and irritable. This parent taught you that the home and family come first — starting with him or her.

LIBRA ON 10th: This parent is charming, diplomatic and puts others first. This parent taught you to be a go-between, an intermediary. Partnership is important to him or her.

TAURUS ON 4th: This parent is stubborn, set in his or her ways, needs a routine, can be indulgent and is possessive. Money is important to him or her.

SCORPIO ON 10th: This parent is controlling, manipulative and secretive. He or she taught you to be in control of your career.

GEMINI ON 4th: This parent is two people in one. He or she is curious, nervous and high strung. He or she may have mixed feelings about home and family.

SAGITTARIUS ON 10th: This parent is generous, outgoing and may tend to exaggerate. He or she is either philosophical or a clown.

CANCER ON 4th: Since Cancer traditionally rules the fourth as well as the mother, this parent is probably the mother. She is sensitive, emotional, very attached to the family and takes things personally.

CAPRICORN ON 10th: Since Capricorn is the natural ruler of the tenth, and the tenth traditionally rules the father, this parent is probably the father. He is conservative, disciplined, stoic, and concerned with what the neighbors will think.

LEO ON 4th: This parent is dramatic and creative and needs to be the center of attention. He or she likes to have fun and loves children.

AQUARIUS ON 10th: This parent is a unique individual who marches to his or her own drumbeat while still functioning according to society's rules. He or she might best be described as **different.**

VIRGO ON 4th: If this parent wakes up in the morning with nothing to worry about, he or she is worried. He or she especially worries about the family. He or she is a perfectionist.

PISCES ON 10th: This parent is either spacey or spiritual. It's hard to get a handle on this parent because you don't see him or her clearly. He or she either copped out or inspired you.

ARIES ON 10th: This parent said to do your thing in your career. He or she is ambitious and impatient and puts himself/herself first.

LIBRA ON 4th: This parent is the family mediator who wants things peaceful in the home. Marriage is important to this parent.

TAURUS ON 10th: This parent's message was to work at something lucrative. He or she is stubborn, indulgent, possessive and needs a routine.

SCORPIO ON 4th: This parent is secretive and controls the family through manipulation.

GEMINI ON 10th: This parent is talkative and gives the impression of being two people in one. He or she looks and acts youthful.

SAGITTARIUS ON 4th: This parent is generous with family members and philosophical about things. He or she may be a clown. While he or she might exaggerate, he or she would not lie.

CANCER ON 10th: This parent is self-protective and strongly attached to the family. He or she is moody and takes things personally.

CAPRICORN ON 4th: This parent is cold and undemonstrative, concerned with appearances and tight with a dollar.

LEO ON 10th: This parent loves the limelight and must be center stage. He, she tends to dramatize things. This parent is also proud of himself/herself.

AQUARIUS ON 4th: This parent found it hard to be a parent since nurturing did not come easily to him or her. He or she is unique and can feel like a square peg in a round hole.

VIRGO ON 10th: This parent is finicky and worries a lot. He or she wants to serve and be needed.

PISCES ON 4th: This parent is a dreamer, an idealist who either inspired you or let you down. He or she is big on make-believe.

Planets in the Fourth and Tenth

Planets in the fourth and tenth tell us more about our parents.

SUN IN 4th: The fourth house is your father rather than your mother, unless the Moon or Pluto is also posited here. You look to your father to fulfill your emotional security needs. His message was that **your home and family should be the center of your life**. Your ego can be wrapped up in providing security for your family. By his presence or absence, he gave you the message that **you are to be the king in your home**. His messages will get stronger as time goes by. The second half of life should be more fulfilling for you than the first.

SUN IN 10th: Unless the Moon and/or Pluto are here, this house is your father. His message was to **be the leader**, be the boss, be on top. He taught you to **be proud of your career**. He may have set the example. This makes it hard for him to take a back seat to you should you begin to surpass him. You will be given power, responsibility and authority in this lifetime. You can easily be in the limelight.

MOON IN 4th: The Moon in the fourth leaves no doubt that the mother rules this house, unless the Sun or Saturn is also here, indicating the possibility that both parents should be read into the fourth. The maternal message was to **find your security in your home** — and with your family — and with her. You may find it difficult to be away from home for too long. You can be very protective of your home and family. Your mother's influence will increase as time goes by, whether or not she is living.

MOON IN 10th: Your mother is the tenth-house parent, unless the Sun or Saturn is here, indicating that both parents are involved in this house. Your mother's message was to **be on top**, to be in

44

charge, and to mother the world in your career. If she did this by example, she will dominate any scene in which she plays a part. She told you to be protective of your career and public image. She may have said that there can be changes in your career and to protect what you've got. You identify personally with your position, career, status or public image. You are strongly attached to being a leader.

MERCURY IN 4th or 10th: This parent is a thinker and may be talkative. He or she is curious and would enjoy travel.

VENUS IN 4th or 10th: This parent is charming and loving, unless Venus is poorly aspected, in which case the parent is self-indulgent and can try to buy your love.

MARS IN 4th or 10th: This parent puts him/herself first. He or she is impatient, aggressive, ambitious and can lose interest in things if rewards are not quickly forthcoming.

JUPITER IN 4th or 10th: This parent is generous and optimistic. While he or she can exaggerate and possibly indulge, he or she is honest.

SATURN IN 4th: You regard this parent as an authority figure. Grandparents can play an important role in your home life. You feel responsible for your family's security. This can make you feel restricted. Your family is run by an authority figure. The fourth-house parent is very disciplined, traditional and can instill fear in you. You may feel responsible for this parent's security and, on some level, responsible for any unhappiness he or she experiences.

SATURN IN 10th: This parent is the authority figure. There is a strong authoritarian note to your upbringing, with grandparents possibly playing an important role. The tenth-house parent is traditional, strict, unbending, distant and powerful. He instills fear in you, which can manifest as respect, since that is what he wants. You feel it is your responsibility to be a leader, yet you may be fearful of being restricted. You like the status and power it brings, though. As a result of being told to take your career seriously and be in a position of power, you may not like doing menial tasks. You may have a dictatorial attitude toward subordinates. You may be involved in real estate or a family business.

URANUS IN 4th or 10th: This parent is very much his or her own person. He or she can be inventive, intuitive, or possibly rebellious. He or she marches to his or her own drumbeat.

NEPTUNE IN 4th or 10th: You do not see this parent clearly. He or she is either an inspiration or a disappointment, spiritual and giving, or martyred and living in a make-believe world. If the latter, he or she can escape into alcohol, drugs, food, etc.

PLUTO IN 4th: There can be a reversal of roles between you and your mother during the second half of life. At this time you will assume the role of controlling parent. Your mother's control over the family is enormous — even if she is no longer living. Your own emotional security need can be fulfilled by being in control of your home and family. Your mother or grandmother rule the fourth if Pluto is here, unless the Sun or Saturn is also here, in which case the father and/or grandfather may be involved as well. You don't really trust your mother.

PLUTO IN 10th: Your mother's message was to **be in control in your career** and be a powerful authority figure. She tries to dominate your public image either by riding your coattails or competing with you for the limelight. You do not trust her. You want to dethrone her and assume leadership yourself. You probably will. She is the out-front parent and rules the tenth house, unless Pluto describes your grandmother, or unless the Sun or Saturn are here, indicating the father's influence as well. There can be a total change in your career at some point in your life. You have a magnetic, compelling public image.

NORTH NODE IN 4th or 10th: This is the parent who will teach you and, thereby help you advance karmically. While you may be tempted to listen to or follow the South Node parent, the influence of the North Node parent will be more beneficial to you.

46

SOUTH NODE IN 4th or 10th: You have already learned a good deal from this parent in past lives. It is time to turn your attention to the North Node parent. There can be disappointment, even losses involved with this parent if you expect too much of him or her.

The Roving Delegates

The signs represent principles to be learned. The house cusp on which a sign falls tells us the area of life in which that principle will be learned. Usually, the principle manifests in more than one area of life, since the ruler, or **roving delegate** of that sign, carries the message to another house.

It makes no difference what sign falls on the cusp in question. We simply link the sign with its ruler's house position. For example, with Virgo on the fourth and Mercury in the eleventh, the ruler of the fourth is in the eleventh. The same thing is true if Taurus is on the fourth and Venus is in the eleventh. The same concept applies in each case.

The house in which the fourth or tenth house ruler falls gives us more information regarding that parent's messages.

RULER OF 4 IN 1: This parent has a direct influence on you, telling you to be yourself, but influencing you to be like him or her. You may look like this parent. Your emotional security need is fulfilled by being yourself.

RULER OF 4 IN 2: This parent influences your values and acts like he or she is your possession. Your emotional security need is fulfilled through money and possessions. This parent may give you money or contribute to your income in some way.

RULER OF 4 IN 3: This parent has a direct influence on your thinking and tells you that your emotional security need will be fulfilled by using your head. Your need for security influences your thinking, making it more emotional than you might realize.

RULER OF 4 IN 4: You have a very strong attachment to home and family. This parent's influence is particularly strong. Emotional security is a big issue with you.

RULER OF 4 IN 5: This parent influences your children and may act like your child. The message is that your security will be fulfilled

47

through your children, through creativity or through fun. He or she may want to have fun with you.

RULER OF 4 IN 6: Your emotional security need is fulfilled through working, serving others and being busy all the time. This parent can influence the kind of work you do — and can even do the work for you. He or she can influence your health as well, giving you the message to be either healthy or unhealthy.

RULER OF 4 IN 7: Your emotional security need is fulfilled through partnership. This parent can influence your spouse and/or choice of spouse. You can marry someone who reminds you of him or her. This parent wants to be treated as an equal.

RULER OF 4 IN 8: You have hang-ups relating to home, family and security as a result of this parent's influence. You, will, however, work through these hang-ups. This parent gave you your sexual attitudes. He or she helps you see the other person's point of view. He or she helps you look beyond the obvious and investigate life's mysteries.

RULER OF 4 IN 9: This parent taught you to open your mind to new ideas, to expand your horizons through study or travel. He or she influences your philosophy of life and attitude toward God.

RULER OF 4 IN 10: This parent either assumed both parental roles or, if other chart indications bear this out, reversed roles with the tenth-house parent. The message is to find your emotional security with either the tenth-house parent or in your career.

RULER OF 4 IN 11: This parent influences your hopes and wishes, as well as your friends. He or she wants to be your friend. Your emotional security needs are fulfilled by being a friend.

RULER OF 4 IN 12: This parent's influence is hidden and difficult to discern. The message is to find security in privacy. He or she could have directed you toward the spiritual, or the make-believe.

RULER OF 10 IN 1: You feel the influence of this parent very strongly. This parent told you to be your own authority figure, but may prevent it by his or her influence.

RULER OF 10 IN 2: This parent influences your values and helps you make money. He or she is your possession. Authority figures influence your values and finances.

RULER OF 10 IN 3: Authority figures and this parent in particular influence your thinking. You think in terms of power, authority and responsibility.

RULER OF 10 IN 4: The authority figure may have reversed roles with the nurturing parent — or may have become more nurturing and caring as time went by. He or she may simply have spent more time at home in his or her later years.

RULER OF 10 IN 5: The authority figure in your life taught you to have fun, be creative and/or have children. This parent may act like your child and may influence your children. You want to have fun and be creative in your career.

RULER OF 10 IN 6: The authority figure in your life taught you to work hard and not just assume command. This parent can influence your work and even work for you. He or she taught you to be either healthy or unhealthy, and can influence your health directly.

RULER OF 10 IN 7: The authority figure in your life acts like your equal. This parent can influence your spouse and/or choice of spouse. You may marry someone who reminds you of him or her.

RULER OF 10 IN 8: You have hang-ups relating to authority and power as a result of this parent's influence. You will work through these hang-ups, however. This parent gave you your sexual attitudes. He or she helps you look beyond the obvious and investigate life's mysteries. He or she helps you deal with joint finances in your career.

RULER OF 10 IN 9: This parent influences your philosophy and attitude toward God. Your philosophy may involve power and authority. He or she taught you to expand your career and your horizons in general through study or travel.

RULER OF 10 IN 10: The authority figure in your life is very important to you, and you are strongly attached to him or her. You are also strongly attached to leadership, responsibility and authority.

RULER OF 10 IN 11: The authority figure in your life taught you to be a friend in your career, but, at the same time, maintain your authority status. This parent wants to be your friend — and wants to be an important friend to you. He or she can influence your friends and choice of friends.

RULER OF 10 IN 12: The influence of the authority figure in your life is hard to detect since it is hidden. He or she taught you to either assume power from behind-the-scenes, or to simply cop out and hide.

MESSAGE
EXAMPLE CHARTS

Couple 1.

Figure 1 belongs to a pretty, energetic young woman with a sparkling personality. At first glance, the Moon in the tenth in Scorpio[2] tells us that the mother is the dominant, out-front parent. Her message is to be noticed, to be on top and to control through manipulation. This is amplified by the square to Pluto and Saturn. This configuration also tells us that the mother was controlled by her mother or family, and she is not a happy person, possibly because partnership is a responsibility (Saturn in the seventh). The Saturn-Moon square also indicates the conflict between mother and daughter (my client), as Saturn rules the interception in her first house. It also tells us that the native may feel responsible for her mother's unhappiness. The Moon-Pluto square indicates that the mother finds it hard to forgive and needs to punish those who have hurt or controlled her. This would be passed along to the native. The Libra Midheaven tells us that the mother's spoken or unspoken message to her daughter is to be a go-between, an intermediary in her career — and to be married. Pluto in the eighth indicates that the client can be controlled by other people's money. This message was given to her by her mother or grandmother. This placement also indicates the strong vengeance which the mother or grandmother taught.

Venus rules the tenth and fifth, and is conjunct the South Node on the twelfth cusp, so another maternal message would be that there can be some sacrifice and even loss in love, but to keep holding on to the dream (Venus sextile Neptune). Venus opposite Uranus says that the mother told her to have fun. This is in contradiction to the Moon-Saturn square, which says to be unhappy, hence a double message is given. Venus trine Pluto and Saturn

---

[2] All example charts are Placidus, Geocentric, Tropical.

says that she can have fulfilling love, but the South Node can still indicate some loss in that area.

The father is the fourth house. His ruler (Mars) is conjunct the Sun (father) and Mercury in the first, telling her to be her own person and assume responsibility (Capricorn) for herself. Since these are intercepted, she may have trouble doing that. Also, Neptune squaring the first house planets makes it hard for her to make progress in self-direction. Since Neptune is involved with guilt, we see that she feels guilty when she asserts herself, when she competes (while Neptune actually squares only Mercury, Mercury is conjunct Mars and the Sun, which draws them into Neptune's influence).

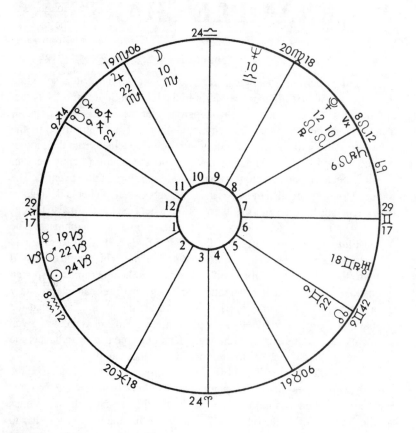

Figure 1. The Wife of Couple #1.

52

The Sun and Saturn are in mutual reception, which, with Saturn in the first, gives her an even greater sense of responsibility and seriousness. It also gives a Sun-Moon square, indicating difficulties between the parents. Since this square is involved with Scorpio and the eighth house, there is a power play between the parents.

Jupiter, ruler of the first, square Pluto indicates a strong power play between the native and her mother. She needs to be in control, but her mother won't let her be free. The need to get back at the mother keeps her locked into combat. Because this is involved with Scorpio and the eighth house, much of this resentment may not be recognized.

Feedback from the client verified that her mother is more obviously controlling than her father (Moon in Scorpio in the tenth), though both control (Sun and Saturn in mutual reception conjunct Pluto). The mother, prior to marriage, was out in the working world and loved it (Moon in the tenth). Yet, she was programmed to get married and have somebody take care of her and pay the bills, so she married. She is not happy (Moon square Saturn), but puts on a happy face (Libra Midheaven). She and her husband are at each other all the time and undermine each other by being negative and critical (Sun square Moon). Her mother's verbal message about love was to **always go along with the man and do whatever he wants** (Sun in seventh by mutual reception) — also to always be pretty or he'll find someone else. In other words, pretend (Venus conjunct South Node conjunct twelfth house cusp). This is in contradiction to the tenth house message that the woman should be noticed, be on top and be number one. How can you be number one when you're supposed to be number two? Another double message from the mother was to eat a lot in order to be healthy, but to stay thin in order to attract and keep a man. These double messages played themselves out in my client's life.

Her father taught her, indirectly, to be her own person and assert herself (Sun, Mars and Mercury in Capricorn in the first). He did this by never really sitting down and talking with her. She had to make her own decisions. He is a humble person who rejects the limelight (Sun square Neptune). He is not talkative, yet corrects his wife whenever she speaks (Sun square Moon). This makes her self-conscious since she is talkative. My client feels the same way her mother does whenever she opens her mouth. She also feels guilty whenever she speaks (Mercury square Neptune) because, while living her mother's message to be out front (the talker is in the limelight and, therefore, has the attention), she is going against her father's message to be humble and inconspicuous (Neptune square the intercepted first house planets). In fact, any time she asserts herself, she feels guilty (Neptune square first house planets). This makes it difficult to play tennis with a male, for instance, and win (Mars square Neptune). Her mother's message is telling her to put the man first, yet be number one. Her father's message is telling her to diffuse her energies and not win, thereby being humble. Her first house says she wants to assert herself, yet the interception and square from Neptune make it difficult.

A guilt trip was also laid on her by her mother who said that children are hard on a marriage (Venus conjunct South Node conjunct twelfth house cusp). This means that my client feels responsible for any unhappiness her mother might experience (Moon square Saturn, Neptune square first house planets). As a result, whenever her parents argue, my client plays go-between, acting as an intermediary (Libra on the Midheaven) between two children, which is the way she sees them. (Midheaven square Pluto equals reversal of roles. Capricorn in the first equals responsibility and maturity.)

Her mother tells her to have fun (Venus opposite Uranus sextile Neptune), but puts a damper on it (Moon square Saturn, Venus conjunct South Node). After awhile, any time she had fun she felt guilty and unhappy.

The mother is unpredictable (Venus opposite Uranus). She goes along with whatever the father wants, then, at the last minute, changes her mind. This controls the situation. My client does the same thing. The message is that **once you commit to something you lose control**, which makes you unhappy, so don't commit.

My client's ex-husband fit beautifully into her programming. He is a very handsome, dynamic individual. His chart (Figure 2) indicates a strong work ethic (packed sixth house) which was ingrained in him by both parents (Sun and Moon in the sixth). In fact, that packed sixth says that all his energies go into his work. His early environment was serious and strict (Saturn and Pluto in the third), and he is torn between doing what he wants to do versus doing what he feels he ought to do (Pluto-Saturn square Jupiter-Venus). Happiness versus responsibility, work versus play. Both parents taught him to work at something in which he believes (Sun and Moon in Sagittarius), yet his father taught him to play as well as work (rulers of the tenth in the fifth). The need to escape into pleasure is very strong (Neptune in the fifth). The mother might be more of a realist than the father (Saturn in the third, Virgo IC equals mother, Pisces MC equals father).

Client feedback verified and amplified the above. As a child he was raised by his serious, religious mother and equally serious, religious aunt (Saturn and Pluto in the third). Therefore, his mother is the heavy. This makes all women the heavy. He was a serious, lonely child (Saturn and

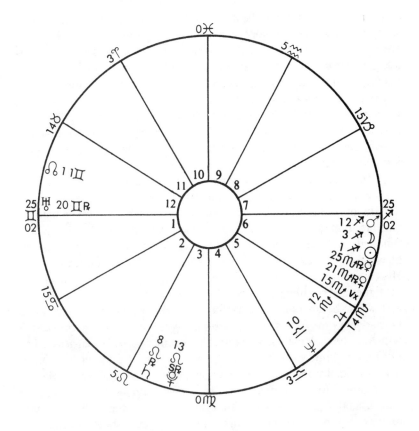

Figure 2. The Ex-Husband of Couple #1.

Pluto in the third). As he got older, he broke loose and went in the opposite direction (Mars opposite Uranus). He adored his father, who was number one to the mother. The mother never complained about the father's being center stage. The father's hobby was acting (tenth house rulers, Neptune and Jupiter, in the fifth), so he was always **on stage**. His father never made it financially and, at some point in his career, developed heart trouble and diabetes (Sun in the sixth of health). This permitted him to justify his mediocrity in business. His father preferred play to work (rulers of the tenth in the fifth). The mother was the heavy; the father was fun and taught his son how to play.

55

From childhood, my client worked — around the house and at outside jobs (packed sixth). His work programming was instilled early and, as time went by, he became a workaholic. Along with that message, though, is the message to be needed (packed sixth, Virgo on the IC). His mother put his father on a pedestal (Saturn in the third equals traditional thinking says the man is number one. Also, Pisces on the MC), and so did he. As a result, he was programmed to have a wife who would do the same for him. His parents loved each other (Venus conjunct Mercury conjunct Sun conjunct Moon) and him, and praised him for his money-making ability. He was loved, not criticized.

This sets the stage for the dynamics of the relationship:

When they married, she put him first, just as her mother had told her to do. He felt she needed him, and this kept him faithful. However, since he was programmed for the woman to be the heavy, and for the man to have fun, and since she was programmed to make believe and go along with what he wanted, yet assert her dominance, this relationship was off to a bad start. His parents never criticized him or each other. His mother went along with his father and put him on a pedestal.

As he became more successful, his world revolved around his work. He had less time for his wife, as a result. When she wanted to discuss this with him, he took it as criticism, making her the heavy. He suggested that, like him, she find something to keep her busy. Her Neptune in the ninth led her to metaphysics. He could not get interested in her world. He was programmed for the woman to be interviewed in **his** world, not the other way around. She was supposed to cater to him, not him to her. When he realized that she did not need him any longer, he found someone else — just as her mother had told her he would if she did not put him first. She played out her double message and lost — just as she was supposed to. Shortly after their divorce he married a self-effacing woman who gave up a big part of her life in order to marry him. My client went on with her metaphysical studies and has gained enormous self-understanding.

Even the most superficial look at their chart comparison shows us how they punched each other's buttons. Her Saturn-Vertex-Pluto on his Saturn-Pluto triggered his **mother is the heavy** message. It also triggered the square to his Jupiter, ruler of his seventh, which indicates trouble in the marriage. Her Neptune on his Neptune reinforced his need to escape through fun. Her Midheaven in his fifth house made her the child and reinforced his need for fun. Her Moon on his Jupiter triggered not only his need for fun, but indicated that they were friends. Her Moon on his Vertex triggered his role in life of being a worker. Her Jupiter conjunct his Mercury triggered his mother's messages, as well as his need to work and be busy. It also triggered his Venus which, while it shows his love for her, also shows his love for work. Her Venus-South Node on his Sun, Moon and Mars not only triggers strong love and sex feelings between them, but punches his parental messages regarding work. Her South Node on his Mars made him feel that no matter how much effort he put into his work, it wasn't enough. Each one's Ascendant on the other's Descendant reinforced the link between them and helped them treat the other as an equal. This went contrary to each one's parental messages since, in his home the father came first, and in hers, the mother did. Her Capricorn planets in his eighth helped him see the other person's values. Her North Node and Uranus in his twelfth reinforced his need to be free.

His Saturn-Pluto on her Vertex-Saturn-Pluto reinforced her feelings of being controlled and, therefore, made her try to gain control through manipulation. His Neptune on hers reinforced her spiritual side. His Jupiter-Vertex on her Moon triggered the mother's message to **be on top**. His Venus-Mercury on her Jupiter tells us that they were friends and shows the love they had for each other, but also triggers the power play with Pluto. His Sun-Moon-Mars on her Venus shows their mutual love and sexual attraction. However, it also triggers her South Node, bringing in the mother's message regarding loss of love and make-believe. His Midheaven in her second says that he influenced her values. His Uranus-North Node in her sixth reinforced her need to be independent in her work.

Even this brief comparison makes it clear that, in spite of the love these two people felt for each other, their programming would not permit them to stay together. She was programmed by a stern father who did not give her attention, which forced her to be independent. This, then, is what she attracted in a husband. His work left little time for her needs. Even when she'd try to discuss things with him, he kept them superficial. This fulfilled her programming which calls for an elusive male who was not interested in her. His work provided his main interest. Her parents criticized each other in order to control, so she, naturally, did the same with her husband. She's programmed for a power play — her competition was his work. She pretended to be happy in order to control. She lived out her double messages.

The problems began when she shifted into second gear and brought the double message into play — when she stopped being a number two and became a number one. His inattention, like her father's, forced her to become independent. He is programmed for the woman to be dependent and need him. She did for awhile, but when she no longer fit his programming, he found someone else who did. He was totally unprepared for an assertive, independent woman. His mother lived her life around his father and let him do whatever he wanted. The father was a martyr, so the son had to be one. My client (his ex-wife) did not appreciate all the hard work he was putting in on the job.

Had she stayed in the number two slot, their marriage might have continued, and she would have been just like her mother — pretending to be happy while waiting for the opportunity to punish him. Fortunately, the loss of her marriage was the springboard to self-analysis and insight into her programming. Her messages are no longer hidden from her.

Couple 2.

Figure 3 belongs to a very bubbly, creative young woman. At first glance we can tell that there was strong maternal programming (Moon in the tenth, Pluto in the fourth), which leads us to ask if the grandmother may have played a role in her upbringing. If so, the mother would be the Moon in the tenth, which gave her the **have a career and be on top** message, and the grandmother would have controlled in the home. Her mother would be a unique individual (Moon in Aquarius) with a strong humanitarian side. The mother's **have a career** message would have contradicted the other maternal message (Pluto in the fourth) which was to stay at home. Saturn on the third indicates early responsibility and the possibility that the native was the oldest, or only child. Saturn and the Moon are in mutual reception, which tells us that she is very emotional in her thinking (Moon on the third cusp) and, while fearful of responsibility, is willing to assume it (Saturn in the tenth). The Saturn-Mars square shows resentment at authority figures. Saturn square Venus by mutual reception says she cannot be happy while her family is unhappy. The Saturn-Venus trine offsets this and helps her find security and love. It also indicates loyalty.

The Sun-Neptune conjunction represents her father, who either taught her to cop out or be very creative. Since this conjunction is square Saturn, we might assume he was of some disappointment to her, which could result in her building a wall around herself (Sun square Saturn) for protection. The mutual reception between Saturn and the Moon gives us a Sun-Moon square, which not only indicates early difficulty between the parents, but sets the stage for problems in her own. Marriage would be important to her, as a Libran, but her dreams (Neptune) would have to fall short (Saturn square Neptune). Her father would have taught her to have fun even behind the scenes at work (Sun conjunct Neptune in the fifth behind the sixth).

Client feedback verifies the strong maternal program. She was raised by her grandmother on her mother's side, while her mother worked (Moon

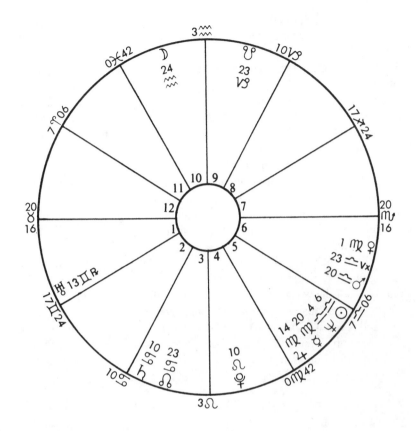

Figure 3. Wife of Couple #2.

in the tenth). Her grandmother's mother also lived with them and ruled the roost (Pluto in the fourth). She is the oldest and, as such, assumed responsibility for her two younger sisters (Saturn conjunct the third cusp). Her mother played the paternal role (Moon in the tenth): working, paying all bills and putting everything in her name. She did this because her husband, my client's father, drank (Sun conjunct Neptune). He was in the motion picture industry (Sun conjunct Neptune) and would disappear for weeks at a time (Neptune), only to turn up in some foreign country. As a child, my client would retrieve him from bars and bring him home. This added to her third house responsibility early in life. She adored her father

59

(Sun conjunct Neptune), but he disappointed her (Saturn square Sun-Neptune, Saturn square Venus by mutual reception). Since her mother hung in there — is still hanging in there — she is programmed to do the same. Her program that **men will disappoint you** (Saturn square Neptune) **and will play** (Sun in the fifth house) **while you work** (Moon in the tenth) was reinforced by her grandfather. She feared him (Saturn conjunct the third) and he drank, too (Sun-Neptune conjunction). He died at the racetrack with his mistress. It's not surprising that my client got a negative message about men. Women were the strong ones according to her programming. She resented her mother for not being there when she was young (Saturn square Mars), and for putting up with her father, but she now understands that someone had to work and assume command. She felt completely loved by her grandmother (Saturn trine Venus), controlled by her great-grandmother (Pluto in the fourth), and disappointed by her father (Sun-Neptune square Saturn).

Her mother gave her the message to do her thing and not stand for the status quo (Uranus in the first), but also to assume responsibility for the family when she wasn't there (Saturn, ruler of the tenth, conjunct the third cusp). Her grandparents taught her to both love and hate work (rulers of the first and seventh in the sixth). Her father taught her to be a martyr and not succeed (Sun conjunct Neptune square Saturn). As a result of her upbringing, the most important thing in the world to her is to be a good mother. While she works part-time, she works out of her home as much as she can so that she can be with her son.

Figure 4 belongs to her husband, a sensitive, kind, introspective man. His family tie is strong, too, as indicated by the Cancer ascendant and the strong fourth-tenth axis. With Pluto in the second, one of the maternal messages was to control with money. The Sun conjunct the third would indicate that his father not only taught him to think, but to feel that his ideas were correct and should be agreed with. Mercury, ruler of the fourth conjunct the Sun from the second indicates that the fourth-house parent taught him to keep some of his ideas to himself and not be talkative. (A third house Sun is not necessarily indicative of a talker, but it does indicate a thinker.) The Sun-Moon square indicates difficulties between the parents at the time of birth. The eleventh house says there is some frustration in the fulfillment of his hopes and wishes, but to go after them. This might have been given to him by his mother, though possibly, with Saturn there, the entire family could be involved. The eleventh house emphasis also indicates that he has always felt different. The tenth-house parent worked hard and was ambitious (Mars in Aries in the tenth), but fell short of his own

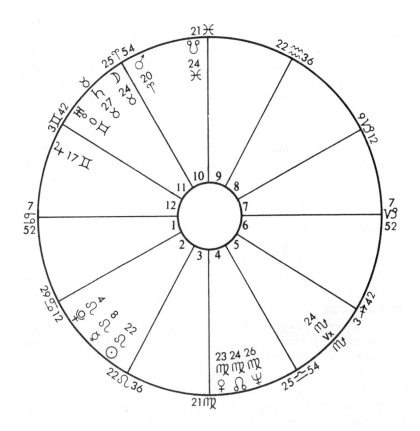

Figure 4. Husband of Couple #2.

expectations (South Node in the tenth). This programmed the native to fall short of expectations in his own career. The fourth-house parent was either an idealist who may have copped out (Neptune) or a truly giving person (Venus conjunct North Node conjunct Neptune). He wants his home to be love-filled (Venus conjunct North Node conjunct Neptune) and, since the North Node is there, it probably will be. With the co-ruler (Jupiter) in the twelfth, there is a tendency for the tenth-house parent to escape, retreat or pull back from life. With the other ruler (Neptune) of the tenth in the fourth, the tenth-house parent might have become more nurturing as time went on, or at least spent more of his time with the family. Both parents were stubborn and fixed in their ways (Sun and Moon in fixed signs).

61

Client feedback verified the above and added that his second-house message about money came from his grandmother who, before her death, said, "I'm leaving you money so you'll remember me." His message is that **women control the money**. This also comes from the fact that his mother inherited some money when he was young, which she used to redecorate the house. This emasculated his father. The fact that his wife (Figure 3) is now decorating their home does not bother him since he is providing the money. His wife, though, says that he prefers it when she spends it on herself. This could be because his mother always spent money on herself, and has an expensive wardrobe. His mother is a southern lady who, nevertheless, encouraged him to do his thing and pursue his own goals (Moon-Saturn-Uranus conjunct in the eleventh). She lives in an idealized world (Venus conjunct North Node conjunct Neptune in the fourth), but he still hopes his own home will be like his dream. The birth of his son probably helped him realize this dream (Venus, ruler of the fifth conjunct Neptune-North Node in the fourth).

The Sun-Moon square manifested as money problems when he was growing up, possibly because of the mother's inheritance and subsequent independence and control.

His father was a thinker (Sun conjunct the third house cusp) who never learned to play. He was cold and unaffectionate (Sun square Saturn). He could not show love. He had a poor self-image (South Node in the tenth) which meant that, no matter how hard he drove himself (Mars in Aries in the tenth), he never achieved what he wanted (South Node in the tenth). He did not have a college degree and was never the business success he would have liked to have been. He was involved in a family business, and would like to have owned his own. He wanted his son, my client, to join the family business, but my client pursued an entirely different career. As a result of his father's poor self-image, my client took years to get his own straightened out. He, like his father, did not make it as he would have liked — until recently. He worked for a company that was not considered as popular as some of its competitors. Recently, they merged with another company, thus achieving status. This made my client proud of his company and himself. It also means he broke through his father's programming. He got beyond it. He is now satisfied in his career, something his father never was. His father escaped into his work, while my client escapes into sleep (Jupiter in the twelfth). When he was young, his parents had friends, but as they got older, their friends became fewer (Saturn in the eleventh). He finds the same thing happening in his own life. As a result of illness, his father spent the last 15 years of his life as a recluse (Jupiter, ruler of the tenth in the twelfth; Neptune, ruler of the tenth in the fourth).

The dynamics of the relationship are as follows:

Since both her grandfather and father drank, and her grandmother and mother put up with it, she is programmed to put up with anything. She is programmed for the man in her life to be weak, avoid responsibility, build up her hopes and then disappoint her. Several years ago, after agreeing to marry her, her now husband called off the wedding a few hours before it was to take place. When he moved across country, she followed and pursued the relationship, refusing to believe it was over. Her husband does not drink, but he escapes through sleep. He also travels in his career.

Her mother's message was to **be in charge** and her grandmother's was to **run the house** — she is in charge of her home and runs it beautifully. She has always wanted marriage, a home and a child. She has all three. She adores being a mother and feels fulfilled in that role. While she is one of the most creative people I have ever known, she has, in the past, been insecure about her ability. She has recently put her creative talents to work in a new career and has already achieved success.

He is programmed for a wife who is a little spacey and simply refuses to see things as they are. His wife's Sun-Neptune conjunction fits that requirement. She refused to believe he would not marry her. The strong female control is evident, as his wife runs the house. He travels a lot, so this is necessary. He has rebelled against his programming by marrying a woman who is not at all concerned about fashion. His mother is very concerned with how she looks. His wife had little money when she was young and holds some resentment against ostentatious wealth. She dresses extremely casually. His mother always spends money on herself. His wife prefers to spend it on the house and their son. She feels uncomfortable spending it on herself. Her parents always argue, so she provokes arguments with her husband. He retreats — her father disappeared. His mother was loving, but his father was cold. He is sensitive, but finds it hard to show affection.

She is renovating and decorating their home. He does not feel threatened by this since he is footing the bill. Her taste is excellent, so he will probably get his dream home. He has rebelled in his career and in his choice of a wife. This has helped him be his own person.

Even a casual glance at their chart comparison is telling. Her Ascendant triggers her eleventh-house **mother message** to do his thing and be different. Her Uranus on his Jupiter upsets his need for privacy. Her Saturn conjunct his Ascendant triggers a fear of responsibility. Her North Node in his first helps him stand on his own two feet, but her South Node in his seventh is not helpful for marriage, making it hard for him to cooperate and give. Her Pluto in his second reinforces his grandmother's message about women, money and control. Her Jupiter square his Jupiter opposite his Midheaven helps him channel his energies into his work (the empty arm of the T-cross is the sixth). Her Mercury conjunct his IC, Venus, North Node and Neptune triggers his dream of the perfect home. Her Sun-Neptune in his fourth also reinforces it, but since they square his Ascendant, they confuse him. Her Mars in his fourth opposite his Mars makes him want to have a home and family, and just as easily makes him want out. It can also take away the energy he might put into his career. Her Venus in his fifth is a lovely placement for romance and children. They had a son, whom they both adore. Her Midheaven in his eighth helps him put himself in the other person's place. It also gives her a good bit of control over their finances. Her Moon opposing his Sun and squaring his Moon-Vertex reinforce the messages in both charts regarding problems in interpersonal relationships.

His Moon-Saturn-Uranus in her first house trigger strong **me-first** messages and make her want to both assume and reject responsibility. His Moon-Saturn-Uranus conjunction square her Moon challenges her role as the authority figure and makes her frustrated. His Jupiter conjunct her Uranus triggers her rebellion and **need to be free**, which is part of her mother's message. His Ascendant conjunct her Saturn reinforces her early message about having to be responsible and in charge. His Pluto conjunct her IC reinforces the **control** message her grandmother gave her, so that he controls her more than she might like. His Sun-Mercury in her fourth make her want a home, but their opposition to her Moon threatens her role as woman-in-charge. His Virgo planets in her fifth trigger her father's message about playing and having fun. They also trigger her desire for a child and possibly cause her to treat him as a child. His Vertex conjunct her seventh shows the karmic tie in the relationship and exerts a control over her. His Midheaven in her eleventh indicates he is an important friend, but his South Node there can reduce her friendship circle. It can also disappoint her hopes and wishes. His Mars in her twelfth opposite her Mars and square her Nodes fires her into action and triggers a strong temper, which can be channeled sexually.

There is much more involved in chart comparison. My point is to illustrate that it takes very little to trigger the other person's parental messages.

Couple 3.

Figure 5 belongs to a pretty, active woman who is always immaculately groomed and fashionably dressed. With the Moon and Pluto in her tenth

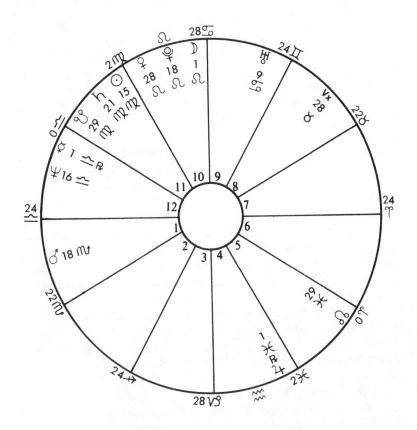

Figure 5. Wife of Couple #3.

house, this house is her mother. The mother's message was to be out front, be on top, be noticed and dramatic — and pretty (Venus in the tenth). The rest of the message is to nurture in her career (Cancer on the Midheaven, Moon in the tenth), and possibly deal with a luxury item (Venus). With the ruler of the Ascendant conjunct Pluto, she wants to be on top and fulfill her mother's message. With Mars square her Venus-Pluto conjunction, while there is love, there may be some resentment at the mother — perhaps for being too dominant. After all, Mars in the first wants to do things its own way — especially Mars in Scorpio.

65

The intercepted ruler of the tenth (Sun) is in the eleventh, indicating that her mother also wanted her to be a friend, and wanted to be her friend. She also gave her the message to be a perfectionist (Virgo). Since the Sun and Saturn co-rule her father, he, too, would have given her the perfectionist message. He would also have given her the message to **be a friend — an important** (Sun, Saturn), **possibly distant** (Saturn) **friend, and to cherish old friends** (Saturn). He, too, would be her friend. His message was also to be the center of attention in a group. The mother added to this message. The Virgo part of the message told her to **tend to the little details** involved in group activities, but to do so from a position of leadership (Sun, Saturn). This would fulfill her emotional security needs (ruler of four in eleven). So her message is to **lead and be a friend**. With the South Node conjunct Saturn, there might be an element of loss involved either with friends or her father, and with Mercury conjunct the South Node on the twelfth cusp, she might not see this clearly. Also, with Neptune conjunct her Ascendant square Uranus, ruler of the interception in her fourth, there is a confused concept of her father. Either he was truly wonderful, or he copped out. In either case, she would not see him clearly. With Uranus, ruler of the fourth in the ninth, her father gave her the message to travel and open her eyes to new ideas. Mars sextile Sun and Saturn says he would have taught her to get along well with men. Mars square Pluto does not help her to get along with female authority figures, since her message is to **be** the female authority figure.

She gave me the following feedback:

When she was growing up, her father traveled a lot and was gone much of the time (Sun conjunct Saturn conjunct South Node). Nevertheless, she has very positive feelings toward him. Her mother was in charge of the home, naturally, when her father was gone. Her mother's career message was a literal one, as her mother had held an executive position of great importance at a time when women did not do that. She defines her mother as being **sweet** (Venus), and wishes she could be like her. I asked her if she held resentment toward her mother, since Mars squares Pluto. At first, the thought that came to mind was that her mother did not insist that her father stay home more. Further questioning revealed that her parents did not want her to marry her husband. They felt he would not be a financial success. For several years after the marriage, her mother would ask her if she were really happy, adding that the only thing she wanted was for her daughter to be happy. This irritated my client because she had to constantly assure her mother that she was, indeed, happy. This constant questioning made my client doubt her own happiness, adding to her discontent. When her child

66

was born, she was truly happy and able to put her mother's mind at ease. She now has no difficulty with her mother. She **does** have difficulty with her mother-in-law, though. There is a definite power play for control over the husband (Mars square Pluto). This went on quite strongly until she had a child. Then her supremacy as the wife and mother was established and eased the competition quite a bit.

Her parents usually agreed on most things. When they did not agree, they dealt with their differences openly. They enjoyed puttering around the house together. To this day, when her father comes to visit, the two of them fix up all the little things around the house that need fixing. Her parents always work around their home as a team.

She has been an airline flight attendant and worked in advertising. She and her husband worked together to build a successful business. With the recent birth of her son, she found her ultimate fulfillment — she is now a mother, and happy in that role. She does not plan to return to the business world any time soon.

Figure 6 is her husband, a successful businessman. This chart is a little confusing, firstly because three of the parental indicators are hidden in the twelfth, making it difficult for the native to see them clearly. Secondly, Neptune squares the Sun, adding to the inability to see himself or his father clearly. Thirdly, the Sun and Saturn are in mutual reception, indicating the interchange between family members and putting the last of the traditional parental indicators in the hidden twelfth. Fourthly, the Sun and Mercury are combust, contributing to the inability of the native to see the father or family clearly. With all that, where do we start? Well, the Moon in the twelfth certainly indicates that the mother had a strong behind-the-scenes role in controlling and restricting, possibly depressing the native (Moon conjunct Saturn conjunct Pluto). In fact, the entire family (Moon-Pluto-Saturn) may have done so, especially grandparents. With the Moon conjunct the Ascendant conjunct Mars, he would have risen on their control and done his own thing. He would probably not have broken loose since the twelfth house planets are conjunct the Ascendant. The tenth-house parent taught him to enjoy his work (Venus, ruler of ten in six), and to be an individual in his career, possibly a pioneer (Uranus in ten). Mercury rules the tenth-house interception and is in the fifth, so that the tenth-house parent would have taught him to have fun, or at least to be creative in his work. (As it happens, his mother is the tenth-house parent. With Mercury conjunct the Sun, this adds to the confusion regarding which parent gave which message.) With the Sun in the fifth, the father taught him to be creative, to be proud of his children and possibly to be a kid. He also gave him the message that he, the father, would be like a child to the native. However, with Neptune square the Sun-Mercury conjunction, the native has a hard time seeing him clearly. Either the father copped out, or is a truly wonderful person, even an inspiration. With the Sun-Saturn mutual reception, there is a strong feeling of guilt and/or doubt regarding the father, which the native might not see. Mars, co-ruler of the fourth in the first says that the fourth-house parent taught him to do his thing and be himself. With Pluto, the other co-ruler of the fourth in the twelfth, this parent taught him to control from behind-the-scenes, and controls him subconsciously. With Jupiter in the fourth, he would have a large home and would love his family. The fourth-house parent would be generous and philosophical. The T-cross formed between Uranus, Mars and Jupiter empties into the seventh, indicating the need for a

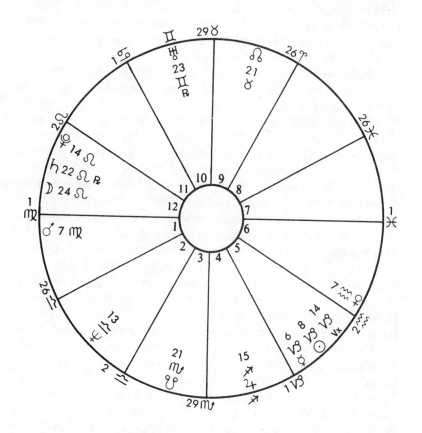

Figure 6. Husband of Couple #3.

68

partner. Since Neptune, ruler of the seventh squares his Sun-Mercury, his partner (wife) would increase the confusion over how he sees his father/ family. With Jupiter, co-ruler of the seventh in the fourth, his wife would give him fulfillment as time went by and, while stirring things up and challenging him (T-cross) could, later on, smooth things over with his mother or family (Jupiter trine his twelfth-house planets).

Feedback was interesting. From what he told me I was able to piece together this pattern:

He has strong family ties, as might be expected with a Capricorn, and his mother's mother is still living, so the twelfth encompasses the entire family. Saturn co-rules the father by mutual reception, so the tendency to be controlled, manipulated and dominated without being aware of it is strong. His mother challenged him to do his best by implying that he might not be able to. He took her up on the challenge and has created a nationally successful business. He feels he's done it himself (Mars in the first).

His father is serious and conservative and, my client, while still a Capricorn, is nevertheless, more creative than his father and willing to take more of a chance. This tells us that his father taught him to be creative by his own lack of creativity. He admires and respects his father, but his father never did things with him as a child, as he would have liked, so the Neptune square manifests on both levels. His father gave him verbal permission to surpass him in his career. This may be one reason why the native admires him so much. However, children set their parents up as their idols and it's hard not to feel some guilt at surpassing them. My client gives his parents a percentage of his business, although they do not need the money at all. He says this is to thank them for backing him financially and emotionally when he was younger. He does not feel it is done out of guilt at having surpassed his father. In essence, he has reversed roles with his parents (Sun in the fifth means the father becomes the son. Saturn in the fifth says the family becomes the child.) He, the successful child, is now the parent figure.

He has an **I'll show you** attitude. He is programmed to prove himself to those who doubt him. This goes back to his mother's challenge that he might not be good enough, might not be a success. At one point, his father wanted him to join the family business. His mother did not want him involved in it. His father put his foot down. This told him that his father thought he was **good enough**, and might have forged a silent allegiance between father and son **against** the mother. This would also have cemented his need to rise above a challenge, which implies he would always need one in order to prove himself. His father's verbal message was to let the woman think she controls things. This incident would have illustrated the father's

69

ultimate control in the home and would have reinforced the son's resistance and attraction to manipulation, controlling women. As it happens, he did not join the family business. Instead, he did it on his own. He showed them.

The dynamics of this relationship are as follows:

Each thinks his family is right. The wife wants a marriage like her parents had, where they did things together, especially around the house. (She and her husband built their business together, but she wants him to feel about their home the way she does — the way her parents do.) While her parents had spats, they had them out in the open and resolved them. For the most part, though, they saw eye-to-eye. His parents often had divergent views, but respected each other's opinions. Yet, they never argued, never resolved their differences. His mother would state her views and his father would let her. The wife finds it easy to find fault with her husband and argues with him. This comes from her mother's message that if things are not perfect, then how can she be happy? The husband lets the wife's complaints roll off his back without responding. This infuriates her. He is getting the divergent opinions for which he is programmed, and she is getting the husband who is there, but isn't really **there**. Remember, her father traveled a lot and she missed having him around. Her husband also travels a lot. When her father returned from a trip, he and her mother would work around the house together. When her husband returns from work or a trip, he wants to relax. He does not enjoy puttering around the house. His father never did that, so he is not programmed for it. He says he now has enough money to pay people to fix up his house, so why should he have to? This is a dig at her concept of enjoyment — it puts her down. The home is a strong bone of contention between them. She wants him to do things her way, and he just lets her carry on — like his father did with his mother. This makes him the martyr. She, in turn, creates the little spats her parents had. Interestingly enough, she and her husband usually agree on the big issues, as her parents did.

He is programmed to rise above a challenge, so he must always have one. He did not graduate from college, yet made a huge success of himself. His mother said he couldn't do it and he proved her wrong. His wife's parents did not want them to marry. They felt he would not succeed. He showed them. He needs someone to tell him he's not good enough, so he can prove them wrong by surpassing their wildest expectations. She constantly compares her husband to her father. This is his current challenge. He refuses to change.

Until the birth of their son, the wife competed with his mother for dominance. This gave the husband two controlling women. The wife feels his family controls him — he puts them up in business, gives them money, etc. She feels that she is being compared to his family. She, in turn, is comparing his family to hers. They each have Mars in the first, so they're both fighters. They're getting exactly what they want.

When we compare their charts we see that her Uranus, Midheaven and Moon trigger his eleventh house, creating the friendship quality she's looking for. Her Moon, Pluto and Venus all trigger his **mommy/family message**, so that she pushes the **subconscious manipulation/control/ restriction** button. Her Sun on his Mars reinforces his need to be first as well as the fight for which he is programmed. Her Sun-Saturn in his first also make him want to be the authority figure, while he, nevertheless, feels her authority restricting him. Her Sun-Saturn trigger a T-cross with his Uranus-Jupiter opposition, the empty arm of which is the seventh house. Add her Jupiter to his seventh and she makes him think of the other person, of partnership. Her South Node on his second, and North Node on his eighth show that they would do well by pooling resources. They were in business together until the birth of their child and did very well financially. Her Mercury-Neptune in his second gave him good money-making ideas, but reinforces his Neptune square Sun-Mercury. This triggers his inability to see his father and himself clearly. Since they were in business together, but since he included his family in their business, you can see where problems arose. Mercury square Mercury also accounts for all the discussions they have, since it is often a question of semantics. They have to repeat and explain their ideas to each other. Her Vertex on his Midheaven shows a strong tie that could be used in business. It also shows that her influence could change or control his career. His mother pushed his father, so this fits. Her Vertex also triggers his tenth house **mother messages**.

His Pluto-Saturn-Moon in her tenth reinforce her mother's message, which is to **be in charge**. This fulfills his need for the woman to be in charge. His Ascendant on her eleventh reinforces the friendship message, but his Mars on her Sun makes her want to assert herself more. It can also make her angry at him, which it often does. It makes her want to fulfill her goals and makes her angry when he is not the friend she would like him to be. His Neptune in her twelfth reinforces the wishful thinking and/or spiritual side of her nature. It also triggers her idealized concept of herself. His nodal placement is the same in her chart as hers is in his, indicating that they do well financially when they help each other. Yet, each feels the other is costing them money. His Jupiter in her second, though, can improve her financial position considerably. His Mercury-Sun-Vertex in her third house make her talkative. They also oppose her Uranus and square her Mercury.

The resulting T-cross empties into her sixth, giving her the need to be busy at all times. She's got lots of nervous energy. So does his mother. His Sun-Mercury trine her Sun does help the relationship and can help them understand each other. His Venus in her fourth gives her a great love of her home. His Midheaven conjunct her Vertex indicates that her role, as well as her joint financial situation, will be under his direction. It can help her put herself in his place and change her value system. It certainly indicates a strong tie between them. His Uranus conjunct her ninth reinforces her need for new experiences. They travel together extensively.

Each one needs to feel that he is right and the other is wrong. Each presented his family in a positive light, for even in this situation they were in competition. While he has not done much self-analysis, she has begun to look at her programming. This has helped her understand the dynamics between them.

A FINAL WORD . . . .

If you've read this far, you've begun to look at your own programming. You've probably relived numerous experiences that you'd thought you'd forgotten. You may be wondering if you are destined, like a hamster on a treadmill, to go 'round and 'round, or if you can get off. The answer is yes, you can. You've already taken the first step by looking at your messages. However, this will not free you. You may stand back with detachment and watch yourself participate in a situation, but as long as you respond to it in any way, you are attached to it, and it controls you. Since our relationships with our families and loved ones are karmic, the chart tells us how our lives will function while we are living under the law of karma. Our next step, then, is to get beyond the law of karma and function under the law of grace. Our ultimate goal is to understand our true identity and simply to BE. If we are being, we are coming from love. When we live and have our being in this pure, unconditional love, our world changes. No one can hurt us. No one can take anything away from us. We have no need, then, to defend ourselves by playing games. We do not respond to manipulation and control from others. We respond only to God (Spirit).

The way to accomplish this is to release our programming and ourselves to God. This does not entail a renunciation of the earth and all the material blessings we enjoy, but an inner surrender, a commitment of the ego self to God.

There are many paths which lead to this ultimate goal, and many books, courses and teachers available to bring you to this point. Ultimately, though, it comes down to your making up your mind that you no longer wish to function under the law of karma — that you wish to transcend it and function under the law of grace. What you do then is simply go within yourself and totally surrender and commit your ego self to God in complete faith and trust unto death. And then wait. You will be shown.

SUGGESTED READINGS

The following are a few of the books which have helped me get beyond my programming. I pass them along to you with the hope that you will enjoy them as much as I have.

Friday, Nancy, **My Mother, My Self**, Delacourte, NY 1977
Friedman, Martha, **Overcoming the Fear of Success**, Seaview Books, NY 1980
Goldstein, Daniel, **The Dance Away Lover**, Ballantine Books, NY 1978
Halpern, Howard M., Ph.D., **Cutting Loose**, Simon & Schuster, NY 1976
Sparkman, R.B., **The Art of Manipulation**, Dial Press, NY 1979

And anything written by:

Joel S. Goldsmith
Emmet Fox
Catherine Ponder
Norman Vincent Peale

ABOUT THE AUTHOR

Maxine Taylor graduated from the University of Florida in 1964, with a B.Ed., and taught high school French for 6 years. In 1969, she was able to obtain a license to practice astrology, thus legalizing the science in Atlanta, Ga. In 1970, she retired from the Atlanta Public School System to devote full time to her private astrology practice. She has been teaching astrology since 1967.

Maxine was one of the original appointees to the Atlanta Board of Astrology Examiners and was a co-founder of both the Atlanta Astrological Society and the Atlanta Institute of Metaphysics.

Maxine has also written, **NOW THAT I'VE CAST IT, WHAT DO I DO WITH IT?, WHAT'S A RELOCATED CHART?, WHAT'S A DIURNAL?,** and **WHAT YOUR ASTROLOGER NEVER TOLD YOU.**